Praise for
The Bipolar Therapist

"*The Bipolar Therapist* takes some of the mystery out of bipolar disorder. Many people fear or are uncomfortable around mentally ill people when they act differently from the norm. By describing her times of madness and her resulting insights, Berger enhances understanding and helps decrease the shame that people with similar challenges often experience. This memoir takes on a serious topic, seasoning it with excitement, humor, and hope."

— Edward M. Hallowell, MD, author of *Because I Come from a Crazy Family: The Making of a Psychiatrist*

"As a psychiatrist working in a hospital that treats people with severe mental illnesses, I can say stigma is a major topic in psychiatry. Bipolar disorder has been gaining more acceptance recently. Yet there's a long way to go before people who have it or another mental illness will get the respect and compassion that people with a physical disease receive. By telling her story in an accessible way in *The Bipolar Therapist*, Berger brilliantly advances this cause."

— Saul Gorman, MD

"Fast-paced and stimulating, a must read! With unflinching honesty, Marcia Naomi Berger recounts in her latest book, *The Bipolar Therapist*, which reads like a novel, her downward spiral into the abyss and her courageous road to recovery."

— Nancy Rosenfeld, co-author of *New Hope for People with Bipolar Disorder*

"As a psychologist who's treated many patients with bipolar disorder, I congratulate Marcia Naomi Berger, LCSW, for writing this book. She shows that people with this illness can conquer its challenges and lead full, multifaceted lives. As more people bypass secrecy and share their mental illness-related journeys, we'll see less shame and more self-acceptance and pride."

— Pamela Butler, PhD, author of Talking to Yourself: How Cognitive Behavioral Therapy Can Change Your Life

"In her well-written book, *The Bipolar Therapist*, Berger shares her struggle with bipolar disorder during her twenties and thirties. By courageously telling her personal triumph over adversity, she addresses the stigma of mental illness. Berger's story assists in the movement to replace prejudice against those with mental illness with respect, compassion, and understanding. Bravo!"

— Linda Bloom, co-author of An End to Arguing

"Marcia Naomi Berger's first-person account of her journey and transformation is courageous. As she writes, 'Someone with mental illness is much bigger and more complex than their diagnosis.'"

— Francis Lu, MD, Kim Professor in Cultural Psychiatry, Emeritus, UC Davis

"Berger's voice is direct, authentic, and spare, yet full of life and intelligence. I am fascinated and uplifted."

— Carol Olicker, MSW

"Berger's compelling memoir lifts the veil hiding the truth about many therapists who we may think are more psychologically healthy than ourselves."

— Francine Falk-Allen, author of Not a Poster Child

"Riveting!"

— Amy Kahn, MSW

"This heartwarming, insightful, and brave story depicts one woman's struggle with and victory over mental illness. Berger inspires us to have hope in the face of seemingly unexplainable symptoms. Beautifully written to touch the soul."

— Lyn Barrett, Author of Crazy: Reclaiming Life from the Shadow of Traumatic Memory

THE
BIPOLAR
THERAPIST

THE BIPOLAR THERAPIST

A JOURNEY FROM MADNESS TO LOVE AND MEANING

A Memoir

MARCIA NAOMI BERGER

Bitachon Press
San Rafael, California

The Bipolar Therapist: A Journey from Madness to Love and Meaning
Marcia Naomi Berger

Bitachon Press, San Rafael, California

979-8-9900275-0-3 Paperback

979-8-9900275-1-0 Electronic Book

Library of Congress Control Number: 2024903508

Publisher's Cataloging-in-Publication data
Names: Berger, Marcia Naomi, author.
Title: The bipolar therapist : a journey from madness to love and meaning , a memoir / Marcia Naomi Berger.
Description: San Rafael, CA: Bitachon Press, 2024.
Identifiers: LCCN: 2024903508 | ISBN: 979-8-9900275-0-3 (paperback) | 979-8-9900275-1-0 (ebook)
Subjects: LCSH Berger, Marcia Naomi--Biography. | Psychotherapists--Biography. | Mentally ill--United States--Biography. | Manic-depressive illness--Biography. | Jews--United States--Biography. | BISAC BIOGRAPHY & AUTOBIOGRAPHY / Memoirs | BIOGRAPHY & AUTOBIOGRAPHY / Jewish | BIOGRAPHY & AUTOBIOGRAPHY / Medical (incl. Patients)
Classification: LCC RC438.6 .B47 2024 | DDC 616.89/0092--dc23

All photos are from the author's personal collection.

Disclaimer: This is a memoir—a personal account of the author's own experience with mental illness. Bipolar disorder is an extremely serious disorder, so please consult your physician or healthcare provider before using any information or anything in this book you may think of as advice. Using ideas in this book is at the sole discretion of the reader. The author and publisher are not liable for any damages resulting from the use of any advice or information in this book. Nevertheless, the author hopes that her story will be helpful to readers on their journeys.

Some details about the author's grandmother, Yetta Herman, are true. Most are imagined, based on the little the author knows about her life. Names and identifying characteristics have been changed to protect the privacy of certain individuals.

Contents

*Whoever survives a test, whatever it may be,
must tell the story. That is his duty.*
—Elie Wiesel

1 – The Anger Workshop

1974. San Francisco, California

Everyone can point to an event that changed their life. The anger workshop was mine. It unleashed something I hadn't known was inside me and turned my life upside down for a decade.

I was twenty-nine and single, working at an alcoholism treatment center in San Francisco during the 1970s. I once joked with our supervising psychiatrist that the place was a day treatment center for staff. He winked, put a finger to his lips, and said, "Shh," as if it were our secret.

The anger workshop revealed the thin line between training and quasi-therapy for staff. The center supported an "anything goes" culture for staff. We were encouraged to get in touch with our feelings, express them, and act them out, no holds barred.

Like me, Carla Peters was a clinical social worker and psychotherapist. She regularly came as a consultant to teach couples and family therapy. Thirty-one and an expert on cutting-edge therapy approaches, she radiated self-confidence. Carla was single and gorgeous, with strawberry-blond hair, a peaches-and-cream complexion, and an Australian accent that charmed me. "Australia is a boy's club," Carla said once. She must have been glad to live in California during feminism's heyday. Today she wore a leather miniskirt and shoes with stacked, wooden heels.

"To help our clients deal with their anger," Carla began, "we need to understand our own anger." I admired her, but what did she mean about being aware of my anger? What anger? I looked around the circle of ten staff members in the barely furnished room and back at Carla.

"This will be an experiential workshop," she said, "and I'll ask a volunteer to role-play with me. But first, I'd like each of you to relax. Close your eyes, and let your mind drift. Then think of someone you're angry with, over something happening now or from way back."

My colleagues and I slumped in our chairs and closed our eyes. This exercise wasn't going to be easy for me. I was interested in hearing about others' anger, but I felt none. I was happy and excited. My sister, Gloria, thirty-one, was getting married in a few days. I'd go home to Rockaway, Queens, New York, for the wedding. I was a bit tired now. My excitement about the trip had kept me awake too long the night before.

Carla said soothingly, "If you're having trouble coming up with anything, that's all right. Just breathe in and out slowly until you feel relaxed, and an image comes to you. Then open your eyes." I filled my lungs and exhaled a few times slowly. I thought, Dad.

Startled, I opened my eyes. Why had *he* come to mind? After my parents divorced when I was thirteen, my father stayed in my life, taking Gloria and me to dinner every week. He often helped me on the phone with math and science homework. After I moved to California, if I returned to visit my mother in Rockaway, Dad and I always got together too. I had stayed overnight with his new family a couple of times. But he'd popped into my mind, even if I couldn't make sense of it.

"Who wants to go first?" Carla asked gently.

I stood and joined her in the center of the circle.

"Good, Marcia," she said. "Thank you, and who are you thinking of?"

I whispered, "My father."

Carla asked me to close my eyes again, take a few deep breaths, remember what made me angry, and recall something he had said. I thought of his critical words and hurtful actions from years back.

"The details don't matter," Carla said. "Feel your feelings, and say what you want to tell him. Imagine he is right here in this room."

Keeping my eyes closed, I said quietly, "I'm furious with you." My voice lacked emotion.

"Louder!" Carla said. "Tell him all about it. He's right here."

"How could you?" I said weakly. Talking to my father this way wasn't easy. While growing up in my family, an unspoken rule was I couldn't be angry.

This wasn't going anywhere. I might not be so angry after all. Maybe someone else should have a turn.

"Take this," Carla said, handing me a hefty pillow. "Beat this on the floor. Bang it and keep going."

I tried again with my eyes closed, but the action felt more floppy than angry. I couldn't rage. I didn't know how. Frustrated, I opened my eyes.

Carla took off a shoe. "This might help," she said, tossing it to me. "Bang it on the floor, hard as you can."

I tapped its heel on the floor lightly, then harder, pounding it repeatedly, panting, sensing the momentum building. I dented the linoleum floor with the shoe's wooden heel. Finally, I banged it violently; the heel detached and flew across the room.

My mouth dropped open. I must have looked guilty because Carla, still composed, said, "Don't worry; I'll get it fixed." I handed her the heel and the rest of her shoe.

"Hmm," she said. "What else is there? Something bigger—"

"How about this?" Ellie offered, pointing to a rickety, old wooden chair in the corner of the room. Ellie, a fifty-nine-year-old recovering alcoholic, was fun, outspoken, and a self-styled hippie who wore her gray-brown hair down to the middle of her back. We were friends and led a therapy group together.

"It's ready to throw out anyway," added June, the head nurse, who was also my buddy. She was pretty and obese but called herself *chubby*, which amused me.

"Are you sure?" Carla asked." A few people nodded, and someone brought me the chair.

I was ready. I let loose in a frenzy, slamming the chair on the floor repeatedly, grunting deep noises from my gut. *Crash!* One of its legs came off. *Bam!* Off came the other. I kept going, bashing what remained of the chair against the floor.

I forgot about everyone in the room, about being there at all, as my rage took over. I was furious with my father. I never told him how I felt about him leaving our family to marry another woman.

The chair's other legs loosened and wobbled. *Smash!* The back broke off from the seat. I stared at the chair's back, still in my hands: a rectangular frame of brown wood with crossbars.

I was breathing heavily, shaking, and crying. Gently, I set the piece on the floor.

"Keep that," someone said. "Take it home."

I was spent physically, frightened, and exhilarated.

Everyone congratulated me. Carla said softly, "This has been a powerful experience for you. It will take time to integrate. Be gentle with yourself over the next few weeks."

Back at my apartment that evening, I leaned the rectangular piece that had been the chair's back against the wall by my closet. It symbolized my father, his hold on me, and my strength, the power deep within me.

I felt drained and proud. I was a heroine!

Me, at the alcoholism treatment center.

2 – Maid of Honor

1974. San Francisco, California

A couple of days before the workshop, I was curled up on my couch, reading *Wuthering Heights*, when my sister phoned from her Manhattan apartment with the surprising news that she and Larry were getting married.

"I know this is last minute; the wedding is next Sunday, during Memorial Day weekend, so I understand if you can't make it."

"Of course, I'm coming!"

"Great. You'll be my maid of honor." Gloria didn't ask; she told me, a birthright she assumed because she was a year and a half older. I had accepted her leadership long ago. I learned important things from Gloria when we were very young, like not to swallow chewing gum.

"It will be a small ceremony in Rabbi Weiss's study." The guests would be our parents and Larry's, Larry's sister and brother-in-law, and a couple of friends. "Afterwards, we'll all have dinner at a restaurant."

Her tone suggested the wedding was no big deal, a formality. She was too much of an introvert to want a big shindig.

I dreaded the thought of my parents at the ceremony. After their divorce, my mother's pinched expression shot through my insides whenever our father came to take Gloria and me out for our weekly dinner.

I supposed the rabbi would do his best to put everyone at ease. He'd been the temple's rabbi for as long as I could remember.

When I met Larry the last time I went to New York, I liked his sincerity and the love in his blue-gray eyes when he looked at my sister. Tonight Gloria sounded happy, and I was thrilled for her.

So I would be maid of honor—*again*. Being the maid of honor at two friends' weddings was the closest I'd come to marriage. Ever since reading an article by Eric Erickson, M.D., while in social work graduate school, I believed marriage was a good idea, in theory. The respected psychoanalyst listed eight phases of life that normal people pass through sequentially. Among these were marriage and parenthood, although he used fancier words. But still single, despite many dates and several relationships, the prospect of my marrying seemed like a distant dream.

"Do you have a dress yet?" I asked Gloria, thinking she'd want a new one.

"I haven't thought about it. You know I hate shopping."

"I have one you might like," I said, forgetting the spats we used to get into as kids about borrowing clothes. When I borrowed a skirt or blouse and returned it with a stain as a teenager, Gloria gave me the silent treatment.

My mother had quoted Shakespeare, probably unaware that his character, Polonius, was portrayed as a fool: "Neither a borrower nor a lender be." She ordered us to stop wearing each other's clothes. "After I'm gone, all you'll have is each other," she added, causing a knot to form in my stomach. I couldn't bear to think of her gone.

"I bought it in Hawaii," I told Gloria. "It's long and elegant, but informal compared to a typical wedding dress. You can try it on when I fly in on Friday. If you don't like it, we can go shopping."

"Sure, bring it," she said. "Thanks. I'll see you in Rockaway."

I had bought the dress two years back, along with two others in the same Kailua-Kona shop. In one week, traveling alone, I visited Oahu, Maui, and the Big Island, enjoying the lush beauty of moist rainforests and tall waterfalls. I saw couples of all ages who looked in love, many honeymooning or celebrating an anniversary.

On the last night of that trip, I splurged on an elegant hotel in Hilo. I sat at the dressing table in my room and saw in its mirror, with surprise, my strained, sad face. My life was all wrong. As though a dam had been unleashed, torrents of tears flooded my cheeks. I feared they'd never stop. When they did, I thought, *I'm twenty-seven. Everyone else has someone. Why not me?* I'd never felt more lonely and cried even more. Finally exhausted, I slept soundly. I flew back to San Francisco the next day, where being single was okay, because so many of us were, and I resumed my everyday life.

Preparing for the wedding, I booked a red-eye to Newark, New Jersey, because the flights to John F. Kennedy Airport, near Rockaway, were full. Its Friday morning arrival would give me a couple of days to relax before the wedding on Sunday.

I put *Wuthering Heights* back into my new, oak bookcase. I'd begun to buy quality furnishings, including a Tiffany-style lamp and an antique, oak commode with brass handles. Both rested on an Oriental-style, mostly red carpet that brightened the room.

Gradually, I'd stopped denying myself small luxuries. I'd held off before, imagining that a terrific man would appear and whisk me off to marital bliss, and we'd shop together for furniture.

Usually, I packed slowly and indecisively, analyzing the likelihood of changing weather conditions, the impression I wanted to make—cute, sexy, or sophisticated—and so on. Now I filled my suitcase quickly and confidently. I was going to my sister's wedding! First, I carefully folded the dress for Gloria and then mine from the same boutique. I tossed in the basics for four days.

On finishing, I felt a momentary sadness. My relationship with Gloria was changing. Before Larry came along, I sometimes imagined us growing old together and keeping in close touch, no matter where we lived. Among our many shared experiences, our parents' divorce bound us. Although we never spoke of it while living under the same roof, it turned out that we had similar fantasies. I called Gloria once from California a couple of years earlier, when I was depressed and crying.

She asked, "Can you think of anything that would help?"

I blurted out, "I wish Mom and Dad would get back together." I felt my face heat up, embarrassed.

Gloria said, "Me too."

We'd both laughed at the absurdity, and I felt better. By then, our father and Ethel had been married for over twelve years, quite happily, according to him. Their daughter, Marla, was eleven.

I stood the suitcase against a wall and turned out the light. Snuggling between my waterbed's satin sheets, I pulled the burgundy velour spread over my neck. The bed's warmth and softness nurtured me.

I pictured Gloria and me in the rabbi's study in our flowing Hawaiian dresses. Mine was a wraparound sheath in sea shades of turquoise and royal blue; hers had a fuller skirt and a swirly, purple and shocking-pink pattern. The bright dresses were perfect for our matching dark-brown hair, eyes, and olive complexions.

Excited, I turned in my bed one way and then the other. Perhaps my body was anticipating changes beyond what my mind could imagine. My thoughts raced: *Gloria is getting married! I'll be there. Flying out Thursday night. So excited. Need to reschedule Friday's appointments. Great dress for her. She'll like it. Want to be there for her. Soon I'll be in Rockaway. Rockaway! The ocean. Like my dress. Gotta sleep. Work tomorrow. Rockaway!*

I tossed and turned. *I'll be okay.* But I hadn't slept, not since the anger workshop. *I'll make it through on adrenaline.*

At the stopover in Chicago, I wandered around the airport feeling enlightened and spiritual. *I'm the Virgin Mary, and I can heal people.* Walking along the corridors, I beamed healing waves to cure anyone whose path crossed mine.

Arriving in Newark, my mother, who had said she'd pick me up, wasn't there. I had her paged, with no response. Unfazed, I felt serene and saw no need to wait around.

I took a bus to Manhattan, the subway to Brooklyn, and finally, the bus to Belle Harbor in Rockaway. At the house, I left a note for my mother: "Everything is okay. I love you. I'm going to the beach."

3 – Delusions

The beach was nearly empty. A couple of people sat on the boardwalk's benches. An occasional sunbather lay on a blanket on the sand, and a few folks walked along the shore.

Late May was early for swimming, but the water was expected to warm up soon. The adventurous would go beyond the breakers. I pictured my mother still swimming way out, her strong arms driving her strokes.

My sleeveless, yellow, wraparound dress wasn't too wrinkled, though I'd worn it all night. Its brightness matched the sunny afternoon. Even though I hadn't slept, I wasn't tired; I was too jazzed to change clothes or bring something to lie on. I wanted to keep moving. I dropped my sandals a few feet from the water, and my feet sank into the shore's oozy mud. Waves washed over my toes. *Perfect. This is why I am here. I am meant to be here right now. All of us are.*

I walked on the firmer sand toward Beach 116th Street, where it was more crowded. My mind jumped from one thing to another.

It feels so good to be in Rockaway again. Gloria is getting married. So glad for her. I like Larry. Soon I'll start my agency. My clients can come for free or pay whatever they want. Money doesn't matter. It will be fantastic because now I always know what to do. I see the inside of people, right into everyone's souls. I'm a healer. Whoever talks to me gets what they need. We all need love. I radiate love and understanding. Like the Beatles song. "All You Need Is Love." I love everyone. Everyone loves me. I can save everyone. I know everything I need to know. I feel wonderful. I love my mother. I accept her. My father too. In her own way, his wife Ethel is okay too. I hope Gloria likes the dress. Of course she will. It was meant for her. I must have known somehow when I bought it, even though I thought it was for me. Everything that happens is meant to happen.

That man I saw far away is getting closer. He is huge. Here he comes: massive arms and a big belly over his skimpy bathing suit. He is drawn to me, feels my energy, and wants more of it. He looks at me. Here he is; we both stop. He looks into my eyes. I feel his soul. He loves me. I feel safe with him; we are on the same wavelength. I beam my energy into him.

"I know you," I said. "We are the same."

"Yes," he said. He stood still, looking kindly, eyes and mouth softly smiling.

He, too, was a healer. It showed in his eyes. I was filled with love for him. His face reflected the radiance I felt inside.

I am causing him to glow, healing him.

He continued to look at me, smiling. His big stomach was firm and proud above his bikini, his face and eyes still soft, but they began to harden. "Come with me," he said. There was a glint in his eyes. "I want to help you."

That sounded strange. I didn't need help; I was fantastic. I sensed he had a plan for me, and I didn't like it.

"I must go," I said, spinning away and walking back the way I'd come. More people lay on blankets and towels and stood with their feet in the water. They've come from as far as the Bronx by subway to the last stop, Beach 116th Street, carrying beach chairs and umbrellas. The huge bikini-clad man had probably been among them before wandering off from the crowd. *Just to meet me.*

I turned to walk back on firmer sand toward my street, confident I wouldn't see him again. But if I did, I'd be okay. I felt serene again, at least on the outside.

My mother is probably home by now. Glad I didn't waste my time waiting for her at the airport. She'll come home and see the note telling her I love her and am at the beach. It will be different with her this time. I will not get annoyed. I will stay centered no matter what she does that could get under my skin. I have grown up—finally.

Near Beach 123rd Street, a man wearing slacks and a plaid sports shirt sat alone on a blanket, reading a book. As I was about to pass by him, he looked up, and our eyes met. Without trying, I beamed into his essence and drew him to me like a magnet. He rose to approach me. He had the clean, good looks I liked: short, wavy, brown hair, smooth skin, was about five-feet-ten, mid-thirties. Lacking a tan, he wasn't a regular at the beach. *He's here today because I am.*

"Hi," he said.

"Hi."

"Something about you made me want to say hello. It's almost like you're glowing."

"Yes. I know." I felt safe with this man. He was shy and serious; he also seemed sincere and respectful.

"Do you live around here?"

"I'm here for my sister's wedding. I'm staying with my mother."

"I'm Jonathan Klein, and I live in Washington, D.C." He said he was visiting his old college roommate for a few days, gesturing toward Belle Harbor. "I thought I'd relax on the beach before he gets home from work." He looked into my eyes and smiled. "I'm glad I did."

A few moments of silence followed. I felt fine, but needed to return to the house. My mother might have come home by now.

"I'm Marcia. I hope you'll have a wonderful life," I said, beaming more healing energy into him. He looked a little depressed, but I felt his radiance, his inner essence, trapped deep inside him. With a bit of help—

"Would you like to have dinner with me?" he asked.

"Tonight's the only time I'm free." I'd be with my father on Saturday evening, and the wedding would be on Sunday. I forgot Gloria was coming by tonight to check out the dress.

A smile of relief broke out on his face. He'd get to spend more time with me. I'd made him happy.

Back at the house, my mother greeted me in the dining room. My note was still on the table, opened.

"Oh, Marcia, what a beautiful note. Thank you." She hugged me, and we kissed. "I'm going to save it. You can include it when you write my memoirs."

Why don't you write your memoirs? I wanted to say, but I couldn't hurt her feelings.

Now she remembered the airport, and her face tightened. *She is afraid I'm upset with her.*

"You don't know what happened. I went to Kennedy Airport instead of Newark, got mixed up and—"

"It's okay, Mom. Really. You don't have to explain; it worked out just fine." *No more playing into her helpless child act. Never again. From now on, we're both adults.*

"Oh, and there was so much traffic, rude drivers honking horns—"

"Mom, I meant what I wrote in the note. I love you. I appreciate everything you've done for me, and from now on I will accept you just as you are and try to be there for you—*always.*"

"Wow! I never thought I'd see the day. You feel like a friend."

Hmm, I'm not sure that quite fits, but—

"How about something to eat? I made a roast and potatoes, salad—"

"I'm fine," I said, though I hadn't eaten all day. "I'm not hungry, and I have a dinner date at seven."

"Marcia, you're as popular as ever."

She likes to think of me that way, maybe identifies with me.

My mother smiled sweetly. "How about a snack, then? Some fruit?"

My mother showed no curiosity about how my date happened. If he was good enough for me, that was good enough for her.

"Thanks, Mom. I'm fine. Not hungry at all." She looked hurt, as always, when I refused her food offerings. I beamed energy toward her and told her how glad I was to be home, and she smiled again.

"You can have my room; I put your suitcase on the bed," she said. Her room was the small one in the back that we used to call "the maid's room," because it might have been used that way by the house's former owners. Our family's bedrooms were upstairs until Mom converted the upstairs into a two-bedroom rental apartment. My old bedroom was a kitchen. Our former den upstairs was now someone's living room.

"Just let me know if you need anything. I know you'll be happier in the bedroom. You like your privacy, and I'm fine sleeping here," she said, gesturing toward a bed near the living room's fireplace.

Although I knew my mother felt rejected when she sensed I wanted to be apart from her, I didn't protest. I couldn't expect much privacy when we were in close quarters. She had a long-standing habit of opening my bedroom door without first knocking and joining in on what were intended to be private conversations between my visiting friends and me as teenagers.

"Thanks, Mom. I'll lie down for a while. Just call me when Jonathan comes—Jonathan Klein."

"Let me know if you need anything."

"Thanks, I will." But I won't. I needed to be alone for a while, but I couldn't say that.

"Thanks for everything, Mom. I love you," I said then and hugged her again.

I lay down and tried to rest, but I was still wired. It felt good to be home in Rockaway, with a date tonight—and soon, Gloria's wedding.

Resting seemed like a good idea. I closed my eyes, but they kept popping open. How did Mom manage with such a small bedroom? Her single bed and dresser barely fit. But she didn't seem to need a lot of space. Maybe she liked it this way after growing up in the orphanage in a room with girls' beds lined up in rows. But I was glad to be in a room with a closed door. Still, I heard my mother rattling pots and pans in the kitchen. Why couldn't she stay still for a while?

My mother's bed was great, like the ones in hospitals with a button you press to raise one end into a backrest. "I like my comfort," she'd said when she bought it.

My mother knocked on the door. I was surprised she hadn't just opened it like she'd often done. "Your company's here!" she called cheerfully through the closed door. I understood. She wanted to get back to Jonathan and enjoy his attention.

His eyes lit up on seeing me.

"Have a good time," my mother said as we left.

When he asked, I suggested Luigi's, an Italian restaurant on Beach 116th Street, a homey place with booths and candles on the tables. It was still light outside, but the restaurant was cozily dark. I felt at ease with Jonathan, like he was an old friend with whom I could talk about anything. I told him about my plan to open a family counseling center and my desire to bring out people's love for each other through my very being and my skills as a psychotherapist. He looked fascinated.

Eventually, when he'd eaten most of his meal, and I'd barely touched mine because I still had no appetite, he asked the question that used to faze me but not now.

"How come you're not married?"

"Oh, my time hasn't come yet, but it will soon. I'm finally ready." I smiled serenely.

He said, "I was always afraid of being confined. I'm a journalist and that can mean traveling. I like the freedom, but . . ." He looked at me with longing, and I wasn't surprised when he said, "I can see myself with you."

Of course you can. I am just what you need to come alive. You're just dreaming, though one never knows. Maybe someday—

"I'd like to see more of you."

I smiled beatifically. "Yes, I'd like that too, but my time is tight on this trip."

"May I write to you?"

I liked that. "Yes, of course. Who knows? Maybe I'll see you in California one of these days."

He was a journalist, in between jobs. He'd said there were too many journalists in Washington, D.C., so he was considering relocating to the West Coast.

We said goodbye on the porch without touching.

Gloria was in the living room waiting for me, looking miffed.

"Hi!" I said, surprised. I had forgotten she was coming but was glad to see her. I hugged her; I was so happy she was getting married.

"So, where's the dress?" Gloria asked. "I've been here for an hour."

"Oh, I can't believe I forgot. I went out to dinner with this guy—"

"I know, Mom told me. The dress . . ."

I got it from my suitcase and held it up. It looked new.

"Nice," she said, seeing its swirly purple and pink pattern. She put it on, and it fit. She smiled. "I'll wear it."

After she left with the dress, I lay down in the small bedroom. I pictured the ceremony in Rabbi Weiss's study, a room lined with bookcases. In the long Hawaiian dresses, Gloria and I would look festive. Dad and Mom would probably rise to the occasion and manage to be in the same room for the ceremony and at the restaurant afterward.

Since moving to California, I hadn't seen Rabbi Weiss, and not often before then. In the past, I'd occasionally gone to services at West End Temple with my mother. My time at its religious school when I was ten was brief. My mother had sometimes used the rabbi as a counselor, venting about her troubled marriage.

After my parents divorced, when I was thirteen, Mom was miserable. She'd told me she'd given my father the best years of her life before he left her for the woman he married. She told me about her sad friends in bad marriages. I never knew people could marry and be happy.

But now I did, thanks to Carla and Al. Carla, my mentor, taught me how to express anger and get it out of my system, as I did with the chair. And Al, my therapist, is so sweet and sensitive. Carla and Al. Carla and Al! Oh, wow. I just realized. They are perfect for each other. They'll get married, I know it. And I'll make it happen just by introducing them to each other. I am so grateful to both of them, and now I will give them the best gift: each other!

Rap, rap! It was late now, and my mother knocked at the door, but I hadn't wanted to answer. I wanted to stay with my thoughts.

"Marcia, are you all right?"

"I'm fine, Mom." *Please go away.*

"I see your light is still on. Can I get you anything?"

"No. I'm okay, just not tired yet."

"Okay. I'm right here if you need anything."

"Thank you. Goodnight."

"Goodnight, sweetie."

Sweetie. Cookie. Her pet names for me, like I was a toddler. I squirmed when she called me by them, but I never objected. After all she'd been through: the orphanage, the divorce . . . let her be.

Alan and Carla. Two people who taught me what my parents couldn't: how to love. How to love myself, all of me, including my anger, and therefore, how to love others. Then I thought of others in my circle of friends and colleagues in California to whom I felt grateful.

My boss, Harry. Once when I was upset about some mistake I'd made at work, instead of rubbing my nose in it, he said I was having "growing pains."

Doreen was another social worker. Bright, pretty, and recently divorced, she'd been the queen bee at the treatment center before I came to work there. I was a bit younger, attractive, and single with no ex-husband-type complications. Also, as the agency's senior social worker, I outranked her, so I understood why she might occasionally and subtly want to undermine me.

Yet when I was depressed, Doreen was there for me. She advised me to wear brighter clothing and told me about a time she felt so awful that she'd been afraid to drive over the Golden Gate Bridge, fearing she would jump off it.

Dina, the occupational therapist at work and now a close friend, said her therapist explained it was natural that she would be lonely in California when all her family lived in New York. Dina wasn't dating now but was optimistic about marrying. She'd said, "You'd better come to my wedding."

Wedding! It kept coming back to that. *The secret of fulfillment is to be married.* My mind kept racing through the night. Instead of sleeping, I jotted my thoughts on a yellow pad. On top of the first page, I wrote: "This is a very important piece of my life's work."

I wrote about the people I was grateful to and kept writing more names, and I wrote about who I loved and others who taught me to love. Tears streamed down with my insights, and I let them flow while I wrote rapidly, trying to move my pen as fast as my thoughts.

As I wrote, I wondered how I could have been so blind not to have seen it. Alan, my therapist, wasn't going to marry Carla. He loved me. He hadn't said it directly, but he'd given hints and signs—like having told me about his separation from his wife and meeting with me alone in the agency's basement where I could yell, and he let me punch his arm to let out some anger. Alan was waiting for me to make the first move. *Poor Alan, so sensitive. He will be hurting until he knows that I love him too.*

Alan loves me. He loves me and has for a long time. That is probably why he got divorced, because it has been me he has wanted all along, but he cannot tell me. That's not allowed for a therapist. So I will tell him when I get back to California. I sobbed, realizing that Alan and I would be together.

Knock, knock! My mother opened the door and saw me sitting on the bed. My eyes were teary; I would marry soon.

"Marcia, you're still awake. I thought I heard some noise in here. I see you've been crying." Her forehead was creased between her brows, and her mouth was puckered. The clock on the dresser said six a.m. She was an early riser.

"Mom." I smiled. "These are happy tears. I'm getting married."

Her face brightened, and she smiled. "That's wonderful," she said, padding toward the kitchen.

4 – Breaking Through

1974. Rockaway, New York

At seven a.m., Saturday morning, I phoned my close friend Marian. She was in San Francisco. I had forgotten about the time difference.

"Hello?" She sounded groggy.

I said, "Everything will be okay for you. I *know*. You *will* get married, and I'll come to your wedding."

"Are you okay?"

"I'm wonderful. I'm glad you're home. I want you to know I love you and that you will be all right."

"Er—thanks. But it's four a.m. now."

I'd been awake since Wednesday. I felt fine, except for pushing away a fear that I'd never feel calm again as my mind kept racing—and where it would take me, I did not know. I was on a wild, run-away, roller-coaster ride, like the colossal one I'd been afraid of as a kid in Coney Island or even the smaller one at Rockaway Playland. How would *this* ride end?

Most of that weekend was a blur. I hadn't slept and was impatient with my mother. When she knocked to check on me, I pleaded, "Please leave me alone." She left, but I waited for the other shoe to drop.

Dad came Saturday evening to take me to a nearby Chinese restaurant. I picked at my food. "I love you," I said truthfully. I was no longer angry beneath a quiet veneer. The old hurts were as gone as the chair I'd demolished at Carla's anger workshop.

So what if I was a bit player in my father's life, while he remained a star in mine? What mattered was that he loved me, and I loved him, and we were both okay underneath it all. He'd always been there for me in a crisis. Anyway, I was an adult now, not a needy child. I supported myself with a good job and didn't need his money.

"I want to pay for your plane fare," he said, taking an envelope from his pocket. He placed it on the table and removed a check. Three hundred dollars.

"Thanks, Dad," I said. "But money isn't important. 'Man cannot live by bread alone.' What matters is *love*, connecting with our insides and other people's insides, to know we're all bound by love."

I ripped the check into little pieces and left them on the table. My father's mouth opened as though to speak; then he closed it and watched me guardedly.

"Daddy, you give me money because that's how you show your love. But the money is not important. What matters is that I know you love me, and I don't need your money. But please, don't ever lock me in the cellar again. Promise."

My father's face looked pained. He remembered what I had long forgotten until it popped out of my mouth. When I was around five, I'd misbehaved somehow, and he'd locked me in the basement. Frightened, I cried, but he didn't let me out for a long time.

"Daddy, it's okay. Just something I remembered. Just don't ever do it again." I didn't want him to suffer. "Daddy, I forgive you. It's okay, and you didn't know how scared I was."

"Marcia, I'm worried about you," he said.

"Really, I'm fine."

"Try to get some rest. Tomorrow is a big day, and you want to be ready."

"Sure, Dad. I'll be fine. Don't worry, because there's nothing wrong. I love you."

Back at the house, I stayed up all night again, and something new happened. I started hearing the voices of people I knew, as though they were speaking on the telephone to me, except they were not. First, I heard Aunt Sally's voice, saying, "I love you. I hear you are having a rough time. Don't worry. You'll be okay."

The phone rang. I knew it was her calling from her retirement apartment in Florida. I answered, "Hello, Aunt Sally," and it *was* her.

In her usual, croaky voice, she asked, "How are you?"

"I love you, Aunt Sally. And thank you for the gloves."

"What?"

"It meant so much to me. I was feeling low, and we were going to the library on Beach 116th Street, and I said my hands were cold. Remember? Last February—when you were visiting. You marched us into the five and ten and bought warm gloves for me. I treasure them. I felt like a little girl being taken care of by her aunt. I love you, Aunt Sally."

"I love you too, honey. Now take care of yourself. I'll be thinking about you." Aunt Sally's voice always cracked when she spoke. I felt her love for me and marveled at what a beautiful person she was inside her stout body, with her broad face and shoulder-length, auburn hair that looked soft and fuzzy in the framed photo of herself she'd sent me, which hung in my apartment. As my mother said, "My sister has a heart of gold."

Next I heard the voice of dad's wife, Ethel, and she sounded different. Instead of saying her usual, curt, "I'll get your father." I heard her say, "I'm thinking about you; I want you to be okay."

I phoned Ethel to tell her I was okay; she shouldn't worry. Besides, I would heal her. She had been diagnosed with breast cancer.

"Are you all right, Marcia?" she asked.

"I am wonderful. And you are just fine too, Ethel. It's all fine. I forgive you. Now I understand. It is all for the best, you marrying Dad and all. And you will get well."

"Uh—your father's not home, but I'll tell him you called."

My mother knocked, and called through the door when I didn't respond.

"Marcia, are you dressed? Your father will drive you to the temple in an hour. Gloria is counting on you. Remember, you're the maid of honor." She sounded falsely cheerful.

"Okay, I'll get dressed." Then I leaned back on the bed's raised part, picked up the yellow pad, and wrote more.

My father came while I was writing about my mother. *Why won't she leave me alone?* I tried to understand why she wouldn't give me any space. Was it the orphanage? That she never knew her father, or was it what happened to her mother? Did she want me to be her mother?

That's it! She wants me to be her mother, to rescue her repeatedly, even though she sabotages me, like with the basketball hoop. When I was sixteen, our neighbor's nervy twelve-year-old twin sons mounted a basketball hoop on our garage without permission. Their garage was next to ours at the end of a shared driveway, but why mess up theirs with a hoop and balls bouncing against it?

My mother had acted so wounded and helpless about the incident that I offered to go with her to talk to the parents. I did the talking while she sat primly on a couch. I explained that it was our property; they had no right and should remove it. Before they could respond, my mother said, "It's okay, I don't mind." I felt like a fool. There were other times too. *She sets me up and—*

Knock. Knock. She opened the door just a bit. "It's time to go. Your father's here. If you get ready quickly, you can go in his car with Gloria and Larry. Or if you need a few minutes more, the ceremony can wait, and I'll drive you. But we can't leave you here alone."

"Alone!" I screamed. "Alone! Why can't you leave me alone? For once in your life!"

She quietly closed the door.

I better get dressed. I slipped into my elegant, sleeveless Hawaiian dress in aqua and royal blues that reminded me of the ocean. I didn't bother to comb my hair or look in the mirror. My mind still raced. I sat on the bed again for the next brain ride.

My father knocked. "Marcia, it's time to go," he said through the closed door. I remembered the basement again and shouted: "How would you like to be locked in the basement? Just tell me that. You should try it. See how it feels."

A few minutes later, my mother opened the door halfway without knocking. "They couldn't wait any longer," she said. "They're on their way to the temple."

"I don't care!" I shouted. She backed out of my way as I blasted out of the room, still in slippers. "I've gotta get out of here!" I raced through the kitchen, dining, and living rooms, out to the porch, and into the street, screaming, "Leave me alone! I HATE you." My mother stared at me from the porch. I didn't want to see her.

"Get away from me. You're destroying me. Don't come near, or there will be trouble!"

Neighbors came out to their porches to see what the commotion was about, but I barely noticed them. I continued to shout at my mother: "Get away from me. I hate you!" An ambulance arrived, along with two police officers. "Let's go for a ride," said one of them. "Okay," I said. "I need to get away from her."

After the ambulance ride, I was taken to a small room. A man in a lab coat, whose expression was somber, asked me the name of the United States president and told me to repeat a long number after he said it. A plump, middle-aged attendant holding a large ring of dangling keys arrived. The man slipped a few papers into a folder and handed it to her. She escorted me upstairs and unlocked a large, metal door, which she locked when we were inside. Her drab, green uniform matched the peeling paint on the walls of the wide, open area we'd entered. She signaled me to wait and brought the folder to a small office to our right.

I turned back to struggle with the metal door's handle. The attendant returned and beckoned me to move away. I followed her into the huge area, devoid of people, except for a woman in a nurse's cap who read charts at a scratched, old wooden desk. Behind her, a sizable, barred window revealed the black night.

The attendant led me past some dormitory-type rooms without doors. Women slept on high metal-framed beds under bright ceiling lights. I saw a bathroom and said I needed to use it. She shrugged and waited outside. I saw everything through a thick, pea-soup, surrealistic haze.

In the bathroom, I saw my period had come. At the chipped, white sink, I was surprised by the haunted face reflected in dim fluorescence, the face of a desperate stranger. My messy hair matched my drained-of-emotion face. They both seemed to belong in this nightmare. But my dress—I also saw in the mirror that I was wearing my beautiful, slightly rumpled Hawaiian ocean dress.

This is all a mistake, I thought, *a bad mistake.*

5 – Too Much Thorazine

1974. Elmhurst Hospital, Queens, New York

Icame out of the women's bathroom, unaware I was in a psychiatric ward at Elmhurst Hospital. The attendant took me to a small room where three massive men were waiting. The one holding a syringe said, "Just stay still for a second, and everything will be okay."

I recognized him. "Let me go! I know who you are. I saw you at the beach. I'd know you anywhere with that huge stomach!" The men laughed. They surrounded me and guided me towards a corner by a large window. *I am Patti Hearst. They are the Symbionese Liberation Army, kidnapping me.* "GET AWAY—STOP! LET ME OUT OF HERE!" I yelled, thrashing about, trying to escape as they closed in. "GET YOUR HANDS OFF ME." Two held me against the wall while the third stuck a needle in my buttock.

I woke up from a stupor or sleep—alone on a mat in a small room with pad-covered walls. I sat up, disoriented. I was still Patti Hearst for a while, but then I drifted back to being a murky version of myself. *Except—I'm pregnant.*

Something inside me felt like a ripe fruit. A baby . . . about to be born. I felt its fullness. I had waited so long, and now—*my baby! It's coming . . .*

It seemed like hours I sat there, feeling the being inside me, so close to coming out, waiting.

Eventually, an attendant arrived. She handed me a pair of green hospital pajamas. A docile, compliant zombie, I put them on in slow motion. Everything was slow.

Like the others, I lined up at the juice station three times a day after hearing my name called. "Aggh!" I said the first time, then spit out the bitter drink. After that, the nurse there watched me closely. The orange juice was spiked with Thorazine.

"Marcia Fisch," a nurse called. Then louder: "Fisch . . . Fisch . . ." until I caught on in my dulled state that it was my name they were calling to drink medicine.

Elmhurst psychiatric staff seemed to believe its crazies needed Thorazine—lots of it—for things to run smoothly.

Eight days of fog. I hung out in a large dayroom with other patients in drab, green pajamas, but most of us were too sedated to relate. We could have been sleepwalking. A TV was on but ignored. We sat on cracked vinyl chairs, looked at worn-out magazines through blurred vision, or stared vacantly.

An attendant with a plastic shower cap covering her hair mopped the floor, leaving a strong ammonia smell. When we heard our names called to line up for "orange juice," we rose robot-like and took the drug-induced, halting little steps toward the table with small, filled paper cups.

I slept in a room with five tall beds and a bright ceiling light that stayed on all night. We were all too heavily medicated to care.

"Please get me out of here," is all I could say to my father when he visited. He looked sad and worried and seemed almost as dazed to see me in this situation as I was from the Thorazine.

But something amazing happened each time he came and we sat together in the day room. I stopped being a zombie. I felt alive.

An attractive young patient, who was not as over-medicated as most of us, remembered these visits when she recognized me at the rehab place we both went to later. "You were so happy to see your father," she said. Then imitating me, she exclaimed: "Oh, Daddy, Daddy, Daddy!" with a big smile and bright, animated face.

My mother didn't visit me at Elmhurst. I think she was afraid to, my screaming at her from her street in Rockaway so fresh. Even in my foggy state, I blamed her for my incarceration.

Near the end of my eight-day nightmare at Elmhurst, an attendant took me to a wood-paneled office off the locked ward. A hospital administrator spoke with my father, who sat across the desk from him. Arrangements were being made to transfer me the next day to Booth Memorial Hospital, a private rehabilitation facility.

Just in time, because the next day I had a scare.

The Thorazine had turned my skin a jaundiced yellow. On my last morning at Elmhurst, I fell forward on my face while walking down the hall, like when a tree falls after a woodchopper shouts, "Timber!" My chin crashed on the linoleum floor, causing shock waves to ripple through my body.

I'd been too heavily drugged to stay upright.

A couple of hours later, my father drove me to Booth Memorial Hospital, also in Queens—but a world apart from Elmhurst.

6 – Booth Memorial

1974. Queens, New York

From the outside, Booth Memorial Hospital looked like a one-story motel. My room was attractive, with two twin beds, floral-patterned bedspreads, matching curtains, and new-looking carpeting.

My roommate, a pleasant, pregnant lady with a Madonna-like smile and who wore stylish clothes, was packing her suitcase when I arrived. She looked comfortably serene. She said she'd been depressed but felt better now. Her husband took her home the following day, and I had the room to myself.

I could use the pay phone in the hall and was free to do whatever I wanted when nothing was scheduled. Patients wore their own clothes, conversed, and participated in planned activities. Between meals, we could help ourselves to drinks and snacks from a refrigerator in the lounge.

People sat, reading or working on crafts projects begun in occupational therapy, which felt like arts and crafts from my camp days. Dr. Barzoni, a tall, balding psychiatrist in his forties, who always wore a suit, stopped the Thorazine to observe me drug-free. My mind began to race again, and I had trouble sleeping.

No longer dulled by medicine, after a couple of days I wondered if I'd been mistaken about Alan wanting to marry me. I phoned him to check it out and tell him about getting hospitalized.

"Alan, this may sound strange, but do you ever think about us getting together?"

"Do you mean *romantically*?" His tone was incredulous.

"I've had a lot of amazing insights lately . . . I was thinking we were going to get married."

"I care about you and am very concerned about what's happening with you. But I have no intention of marrying you. Our relationship is professional."

"I guess my mind was playing tricks on me."

It was as though the air had puffed out of my balloon. But I was glad I talked to him. *Now that's cleared up, anyway. Except, maybe he's not aware yet that we belong together. Or thinks he should wait to tell me what I'm sensing is real.*

No. I think Al's telling the truth. I needed to accept that. I felt foolish but also glad to have closure so I could move on.

I still had plenty going for me, especially in my career. The words of a song Judy Collins recorded ran through my mind. I was starting to look at life from both sides. Until then, I'd been viewing patients from the outside.

Many outpatients I saw at my job had been inpatients for detoxification and rehabilitation. At Booth Memorial, I gained an understanding of what it was like to be a psychiatric inpatient. Most professionals never had this kind of experience. Now that I'd seen life from both sides, I was eager to be back at work with my new perspective.

I took a leadership role in the daily community meetings at Booth Memorial. I drew patients out about their concerns and offered suggestions. We had had community meetings for our inpatients at the alcoholism treatment center. I was in my element and shone.

But I longed to return to California. First, I needed to face two problems. Dr. Barzoni refused to discharge me after a week, when I felt ready to leave. Enough Thorazine had left my system for me to feel normal, except for the second problem: my mind was racing and keeping me awake at night. After what happened following my sleepless nights before Elmhurst, I was petrified of not sleeping.

One night around midnight, I walked to the office at the end of the hall. It felt warm and inviting, with curtains in a cheerful, abstract pattern. A clean-cut, young man in a short-sleeved, button-down shirt sat reading at a desk on which sat a vase of red and white carnations. He looked up when I came in.

"I can't fall asleep," I said.

"That happens sometimes. Maybe you want to talk?"

"I don't need to talk. I need to get out of here."

"You need to get well first."

"But I'm not sick! My mother is the sick one. She called the police to get me locked up in that Elmhurst snake pit. I finally found my true self, and she couldn't take it when I got so fed up with her that I ran out to the street, screaming."

"You can talk to your doctor about that tomorrow. Why don't you try to sleep now?"

"I can't. My mind keeps jumping around."

"Maybe you'd like to go to the lounge. You could watch television, read, work on a crafts project . . ."

"A crafts project, hmm . . . I started weaving on a loom yesterday." I liked the repetitive movement's steadying effect as I weaved the wool back and forth to create woof and warp. "I always loved arts and crafts as a kid at camp."

"Me too." He looked sweet, with curly, blond hair and cheeks that puffed out when he smiled.

"You look young to be working here," I said.

"It's a good job for me. I go to college during the day. I'm a psych major."

"I was an English major."

I'd left my weaving on a table in the corner of the lounge near bins of crafts supplies. I had been making a flat piece of dark-green, russet, and taupe fabric, with one thick stripe of each color, keeping my hands busy and calming my mind.

Back in the lounge, curled up on a couch and continuing to add rows, I realized I could turn this into a pillow. My mind slowed and relaxed as I wove. The wool felt crisp and satisfying against my skin; I liked feeling the emerging fabric.

My thoughts drifted to my life in San Francisco. I yearned to return to my apartment, bed, kitchen table, and other things. I wanted to go back to my friends and my job. I pictured my boss, Harry, whom I'd phoned the day before. He said, "Take as long as you need; your job will be waiting for you." *What a guy!* It never occurred to me that coworkers might stigmatize me.

At about one a.m., I made hot chocolate in the lounge's kitchenette, then returned to weaving. The finished pillow had fringes and three broad stripes of rich colors—It was a nice size to wrap my arms around. I took it to bed and drifted into sleep.

Dr. Barzoni talked with me for about fifteen minutes daily. He said my mother called to see how I was doing.

"I don't want to see her."

"Yes," he said. "I think it is wise to avoid contact with her for now. I explained this to her."

"I need to leave. I have a job to return to, clients I need to see."

"Yes, I know you don't feel you need to be here. But we want to make sure you're stable before discharging you. It takes several days to clear out the effects of Thorazine. Then we want to see you free of medication for a week and go from there."

I sighed, then began to cry. He looked at me with understanding, but I wanted more than that. I wanted my life back.

"There's nothing wrong with me," I said hopelessly, knowing how things stood. "I just hadn't slept enough. Then my mother did her number on me, and I got so mad at her. I ran outside and screamed. She was scared, I guess, so she called the police. But she didn't care about what happened to me. This whole mess is because of her.

"And she's still butting into my life, aggh! I learned she called the alcoholism center where I work and said I had the flu. My mother contacted them and lied about me. I'm twenty-nine years old. She sent my landlady a check for the rent. She assumes I don't know enough to send in my rent. That's how she's always treated me."

"Had she discussed this with you before deciding to do it?"

"I heard from other people that she did it. By then, the Thorazine had worn off and I'd already called my boss, told him the truth, and sent my landlady a check. I can take care of myself, but she treats me like I'm two years old."

Dr. Barzoni listened seriously and made no comment.

"I'm stuck here for no reason except that my mother made it happen. Wasn't eight days in the snake pit enough?"

The next day a get-well card arrived from my mother. Suddenly I understood: She was sick but wanted to pretend it was me. She wanted me locked up for life, like her mother was. Then she could feel sorry for me and tell her friends: "Poor Marcia . . . just like her grandmother . . . mentally ill, you know." I shredded the card into tiny pieces. Had it not been for Dad, would my fate have been similar to my grandmother's, who died at age eighty at Rockland State Hospital?

That night I had trouble sleeping again. Frustrated, I walked to the office with my new pillow.

A kindly, gray-haired nursing assistant was on duty. She wore a white hospital jacket over a peach summer skirt and blouse. Some of the flowers in the vase were starting to wilt, but they still added cheer to the room.

"What a lovely pillow," she said.

"Thanks. I made it." She raised her eyebrows, impressed.

"I can't sleep," I said.

"A hot bath helps many people," she smiled. "I like them myself."

"A hot bath … maybe …"

As a child, I'd enjoyed many baths in the upstairs bathroom by my bedroom in Rockaway. I became used to functional, quick showers in my college dorm, a pattern I continued until now. A bath. Why not?

I filled the tub, soaked, and let the hot water envelop me for a long time before toweling myself dry in the steamy room.

That night I slept while hugging my new pillow. Two significant pillows so far. The first was the one I hit the floor with at the anger workshop. I didn't know a third pillow awaited me.

I missed my apartment. I imagined sinking into the softness of my waterbed, snuggling under the soft turquoise, pink, and white quilt. I'd bought it at a Tahoe City shop near Olympic Valley, where a group of us rented a cabin for the season and skied at Palisades Tahoe. A local woman made the quilt, which made it especially lovely.

I pictured the rocking chair near my bed, an early American reproduction with floral-patterned cushions. People were smaller back then, so the chair perfectly fit my five-foot-four frame. I first saw it at Sturbridge Village, a recreated eighteenth- and nineteenth-century town that Gloria and I visited last year. Back in San Francisco, I'd bought it from the catalog I took home.

7 – Release

1974. Booth Memorial Hospital, Queens, New York

"We're going to start you on Prolixin today," said Dr. Barzoni. "It should help you sleep better and slow down your thoughts." I was apprehensive. After a week off Thorazine, I felt alive again and wanted to keep it that way.

"Prolixin?"

"It's a combination of an antidepressant and an antipsychotic."

An *antipsychotic*. "Like Thorazine?"

"It's different, much milder. You may not feel any effect for a few days until it builds up in your system. We want to make sure you'll be okay when you get out; we don't want you having a relapse."

"Okay." I trusted him and liked his directness. Beneath his professional demeanor, I sensed concern and competence. Besides, he'd said, "When you get out."

I felt joyous as his words sunk in.

"I've arranged for you to have a pass to go out with your father tomorrow. See how you feel out in the world again. How does that sound?"

My smile said it all.

My father brought Amy. We had been close ever since meeting in our seventh-grade classroom in Rockaway. She was single and lived in Brooklyn. When Amy visited me in San Francisco a couple of years before, we'd gone sightseeing and shopping. I bought my handmade Red Riding Hood doll from a street vendor at Fisherman's Wharf. It became a grandma when turned upside down, and a wolf's face is under the grandma's cap. Amy and I felt risqué that day, buying bikini bathing suits at a Polk Street shop famous for its collection.

*My changeling
Red Riding Hood doll.*

[photo credit: Abraham Berger]

After I hugged them, Dad asked where I'd like to go for lunch.

I could almost hear my heart saying where I craved to be, where I could breathe.

"How about the boardwalk in Rockaway?" I said while the air fanned my face through the car's open window. I turned to my friend in the back seat.

"Amy, I'm so glad to see you."

"Me too, you." She smiled. "You look good."

Was she surprised? I wondered what she expected to see. She looked lovely, much like when we first met as girls. Her sweet, shy smile lit up her soft features, framed by shoulder-length, light-brown hair.

"This has been an ordeal, but I'm really fine. The whole thing was a big mistake. They should never have put me in that Elmhurst snake pit."

Dad kept his eyes on the road. Amy shook her head, commiserating.

"Mm," I said, inhaling Rockaway's salty air as we walked up the boardwalk's ramp on Beach 126th Street. As we headed toward Beach 116th Street, we passed brick apartment buildings lined up on our left. The pale, flesh-colored sand on our right seemed to stretch to infinity.

"Not too crowded," observed my father.

"The kids are still in school, Dad. They'll be out in a week, and it will look different." I hadn't lost track of time. One of the routines at our community meetings at Booth Memorial was to note the date on the large posted calendar.

He nodded. I realized he'd taken the day off from his high school principal job to see me.

"Dad, you are so good to me. Thanks for doing this. And for bringing Amy. I feel like a little girl with her daddy and my good friend. I love you both."

"I love you too," my father said.

Amy smiled a bit nervously. Had she been tense about how to respond to me as a psychiatric inpatient? Or had Amy, like the old me, been uncomfortable hearing or expressing strong feelings with a friend? Even though she was my best friend back then, I hadn't revealed my parents' divorce to her when I was thirteen. And when her mother died three years later, she hadn't told me. I still hadn't mentioned the divorce. Of course, she knew, as word got around.

But I was changing, and it felt good.

My father slowed as though he wanted to watch seagulls eating food scraps on the sand, falling back a polite distance behind us.

"You've been through a lot," Amy said, offering me an opening tactfully.

"Amy, I am so glad we're still close. And it wouldn't have happened without Mrs. Pennett." We both smiled, remembering our seventh-grade teacher together.

"And because of you, I didn't get an 'A' in Conduct for the first time. Mrs. Pennett gave me a 'B' because I talked to you too much during class."

"Yeah, I'd always been quiet until seventh grade, when my desk was next to chatty Marlene Feldman's. That got me a 'D' in Conduct because I talked so much to her. But it also gave Mrs. Pennett the idea to move me to a desk next to yours." Amy smiled. "My mother liked that 'D.' On earlier report cards, my teachers gave me an 'A' but wrote I was 'too quiet.' You helped end all that—all those school projects we did together. Bowling. Going for square pizza near where you moved to in Brooklyn—"

"Don't forget the Columbia Dances we used to go to, the subway rides late at night, you staying over at my house in Brooklyn after—"

"How could I forget? That's how I met my Mormon boyfriend from Utah. A freshman at Columbia, he took me to his fraternity's Sweetheart of Sigma Chi party when I was a senior in high school."

Me, during my college years.

After college Amy and I were roommates at the University of Michigan, where we both earned master's degrees in social work. She now worked at a senior center in Manhattan, which she liked, except everyone knew her supervisor was *psychotic*.

Psychotic. Is that how people would refer to me?

"I have a wonderful boss. He said to take as much time off as I needed. I'm fortunate he's so understanding and accepting. He respects me, even referred a couple to me for marriage counseling."

Amy nodded. I sensed she might not know whether to believe this.

"Anybody hungry yet?" Dad asked, catching up.

As we approached Beach 116th Street, we were quieter now, each in our own world of sand, seagulls, and a horizon where the ocean and sky met in a shade of the palest blue.

We decided on Luigi's for lunch, where I'd gone with Jonathan Klein, the journalist I'd met on the beach. After all I'd been through since then, that seemed like a long time ago. No candles this time; enough sunlight filtered into our booth to see each other clearly. Amy went to the restroom after the waiter took our orders.

My father looked concerned.

"Dad, I'm fine now. Really. The whole thing is a mistake. It was the Thorazine that was the real problem. Eight days! A nightmare."

"It's unfortunate that when you went there, most doctors were off because it was Memorial Day weekend. They had a skeleton crew."

"But what about after the weekend?"

My father shook his head as though to say this was a mystery to him, but I wanted to understand what happened.

"I went in on a Sunday night. Wasn't the staffing back to normal by Tuesday? Why did they leave me so doped up for so long? Why didn't they let me out sooner?"

"This is awkward." He looked troubled and sipped water. "They wanted to start planning to get you out, but when they told Mollie they were ready to transfer you to an appropriate facility, and she'd have to pay for your stay there, she told them she didn't have the money."

I gasped, incredulous.

"She said she wouldn't pay?" My mouth dropped open. She could have found a way. "That last day—when I fell, I could have—"

"When the doctor explained, I said I'd take care of the money. Uncle Marty came up with the place and made sure there was a bed for you. He knew someone who knew the director at Booth Memorial."

Dad's brother was a psychologist and the director of a Brooklyn teaching clinic, and he had many connections. He might have saved my life. I also felt deeply grateful to my father.

"Oh, Dad, if it wasn't for you . . . I'll pay you back."

"Don't worry about it."

"The main thing is that you're getting better," he said, regarding me levelly. "Dr. Barzoni said he thinks pretty soon—"

"I was ready as soon as they stopped drugging me. They should never have put me in a hospital. I was pretty upset but would have gotten over it if I'd been left alone."

"In all fairness—"

"Fairness, nothing!"

I knew he felt sorry for my mother. But she had me locked up and would have thrown away the key. That's what it came down to. I viewed my mother as grossly irresponsible. She'd caused me to get trapped in that horrible place and then refused to help get me released from it.

But I didn't say that to my father. He would have shrugged his shoulders and given me a look to say she couldn't help it, and I'd feel like I was supposed to think, *poor Mom*, but I didn't want to feel that now. I needed to get out of this mess and go home to California.

My father looked at me strangely. I hadn't meant to get upset or to upset him. I carefully arranged my napkin on my lap.

"Dad, the main thing is that I'm okay now. You can see that, can't you, that I'm okay?"

He paused, then said, "To tell you the truth, I'm not sure."

"What do you mean? I'm my regular self, but even better. I feel so good and can hardly wait to get back to work. I felt like I was working when I led a community meeting for patients the other day."

"Your eyes look different."

"Different?"

"They look," and he paused, "glazed."

Glazed? *Crazed?* I'd never felt saner. I felt happy and alive. Was he so used to seeing me repressed that he confused aliveness with crazy?

"Dad, this is the real me. It's like I've never felt so strong and sure of myself before."

He nodded but didn't look convinced. We stopped talking when Amy returned and slid beside me in the booth.

"Have you seen Gloria?" Amy asked.

"She and Larry came by a few days ago. They looked happy." I had told them how sorry I was about missing their wedding. They made light of it and seemed more concerned for me.

The waiter arrived with plates of pasta and salads, safe topics for our next conversation.

Two weeks after my admission, Dr. Barzoni arranged for my release. My discharge papers showed no diagnosis. That came later.

8 – Parents' Divorce

1974. Flying to San Francisco, California

During the trip back to California, I continued crocheting a wool scarf I'd started after finishing the pillow. We stopped in Chicago again, but I stayed on the plane and kept to myself, unable to shake a sense of outrage that my mother would have left me in a psych hospital forever. I knew I would not speak to her for a long, long time.

I dropped a stitch, and had to backtrack.

Until now, estrangement from her would have been unthinkable. In the back of my mind, had always been the thought, *Poor Mom. She wasn't mothered at all. Or fathered. And then her husband—my father—left her.*

An image of the antique spinning wheel from our Rockaway home appeared. I had stared at it while my parents told us they were separating. That night, in an attempt to console me, she first told me about the orphanage.

1957. Rockaway, New York

My mother had agreed to move from Brooklyn to Rockaway, hoping to satisfy my father's restlessness. She probably would have agreed to almost anything to save her marriage, though my father had checked out of it long ago.

Dad was rarely home for dinner. After teaching radio repair all day at George Westinghouse Vocational High School, he went to his evening job as a technology magazine editor. Once home, Dad would retreat to his basement workshop. He sometimes left for a weekend during winter—to go skiing, he said.

Maybe I hadn't noticed my father's unhappiness because he spent so little time with us. Even though our whole family skied, I never questioned our father's taking off alone. Nor did my mother.

"I was a mouse," she said.

We must have all viewed him like a king, not to be questioned, glad to have him with us—three blind mice. If signs pointed to a less-than-perfect marriage between my parents, I hadn't noticed them.

My mother had shared blissful memories of their courtship, including when she introduced my father to skiing. She said, "Your father and I met in a class for teachers when we had just begun teaching. We were lucky to have good jobs during the Depression."

A framed photo showed the two of them looking like movie stars. My mother, smiling; her heart-shaped face radiating sweetness. She wore her shoulder-length, dark-brown hair in a popular 1940s style, the ends curving into a roll. My father's hair was dark and wavy. His brown eyes gleamed as he smiled confidently, his fedora tipped at a rakish angle. They both looked trim and fit.

"I knew I loved him because I couldn't stop thinking about him," my mother told me. "I would walk down the street thinking, 'Oscar, Oscar, Oscar.' And he said he was thinking, 'Mollie, Mollie, Mollie.' After a year of Sunday outings, he asked me, 'When are we going to get married?' Everyone said we were the perfect couple."

My mother on her wedding day.

I was nine and crying in the car as we followed the moving van to Rockaway. I loved hanging out with kids on the stoops in front of our Brooklyn house. I would miss my friends and teacher at school, and the corner store where I could walk on my own to buy an ice-cream cone.

Rockaway's boardwalk began two blocks from our new house. Gloria and I, covered with baby oil to help us tan, a common practice back then, walked along the shore's wet sand in the summer, letting the tide wash our feet.

Sometimes we went out far enough to let the waves bob us up and down. I made sure my feet could return to the ocean floor, kept my head above the water and rushed toward the shore when a big wave threatened to break and submerge me. The dreaded undertow lurked in the background, and I imagined being swept out to a place of no return. Our athletic parents hadn't worried about that; they swam way out beyond the breakers.

We walked our little dog, Candy, to the empty lots near our street. But I first took Rockaway's pleasures for granted, because I still longed for Brooklyn.

A year or so later, I felt at home in Rockaway. Until the day everything changed. I remember sunlight streamed through venetian blinds, brightening our living room. I sat curled up in a rust-colored easy chair, snug against its nubby fabric, legs bent underneath me, engrossed in a Nancy Drew mystery. Gloria read a book in a matching chair.

Our parents came in from the kitchen looking grim. "We have something to tell you," Dad said. They sat on straight-backed chairs facing ours. Mom had a deep crease between her brows. My father spoke slowly, deliberately, as though he had rehearsed this scene and the curtain had risen.

"Your mother and I have not been getting along for some time," he said in a gravelly voice. His body trembled slightly, something I'd never seen before. He shifted an unlit pipe from one hand to the other. I smelled the familiar tobacco odor.

What's he talking about? I thought. I never saw anything wrong. Dad's home late most evenings, but that's because of his editing job. I gazed toward the antique spinning wheel in front of the red-brick fireplace.

"We tried for a long time to make it work. I'll move to an apartment on Kings Highway in Brooklyn. It's only about twenty minutes from here. I'll come to see you every week."

The creases between Mom's eyebrows deepened. She could have added that she wished she could snap my father out of his delusion that he would be happier without her.

A *trial separation*, they called it.

Gloria and I burst into tears. Our parents rushed to us. Dad held me in his arms while Mom comforted Gloria. We stayed this way for a long time until the room darkened.

Later that evening, my mother came to my room as I lay in bed, my pillow wet with tears. She opened the door a crack and whispered, "Marcia?" I sniffled. She lay beside me under my pink chenille bedspread. The warmth of her body soothed me.

"Would you like me to tell you about when I was a young girl?" she asked.

If she was trying to distract me, it worked. "Mm-hm," I nodded, although the room was too dark to see.

My mother had lived in an orphanage from when she was a few months old, though when she talked about her childhood back then, it sounded like a fairy tale. As she told her story, I desperately wanted to escape into another world that would make me forget mine.

"When I was four, I learned I had a sister," my mother began. "I was playing outside with the younger girls in a small yard. One of the older girls playing on the other side of the fence tossed an orange over to me. I ran to see who it was. She gave me a big smile and said, 'I'm your sister.' I wanted to hug her, but there was that fence between us. That was your Aunt Sally; she was called *Sadie* back then. Oh, I was thrilled to have a sister."

Lucky Mom.

I thought of Aunt Sally, her husband, Uncle John, and my cousin Margaret, who lived on their farm in upstate New York. Gloria and I were city girls; we held our noses to avoid the stench of barnyard animals and gagged at the taste of warm milk taken from a cow that day. I couldn't picture my tall, stout, auburn-haired Aunt Sally as an eight-year-old.

My mother's tone sharpened as she recalled bitter times. "Ignorant young women worked at the Academy.[1] They thought

---

1   The "Academy" was an upscale name many people used for the Hebrew Orphan Asylum, or the H.O.A.

it was funny to scare us at night when we were in bed. They made spooky noises, like 'hoooh, hoooh, hoooh,' and sometimes shrieking sounds that hurt my ears. I used to hide my head under the covers, afraid to make a sound."

Poor Mom.

I pictured my mother alone in bed, quivering under her blanket in a large room filled with little girls.

"They didn't give us snacks between meals, so sometimes we went hungry. But then something wonderful happened," my mother says, her voice animated. "When I was nine, I was given a job selling candy at the orphanage. I made money and got to eat candy!"

Lucky Mom.

"I chose a girl to help me sell candy so I could take breaks. That was Esther, your 'Aunt Esther.' We're still close after all these years."

No snacks. My mother was a hungry little girl. Our refrigerator was so crammed that I was often frustrated when looking for something—usually, some food rotted because there was too much to keep track of. But my mother needed vast amounts of food on hand. Her formerly trim body was now overweight. But still, she was hungry.

The night my father said he was moving out, my parents called it a *trial separation.* Perhaps my mother believed it was, but they divorced within six months, when I was thirteen. Years later, she told me, "For years, your father said he was unhappy and was staying 'because of the children.' I didn't believe he wanted to leave."

As I lay in bed that night with my mother, I did believe it was a trial separation. I listened to her orphanage stories, fascinated. I stopped crying and let myself drift into her story, which, superimposed on mine, left no room for my pain.

9 – Yetta and Morris

1974. Flight to San Francisco, California

During my teenage years, I learned more about the lives of my mother and grandmother, whom I never met. My mother never spoke of her mother, Yetta Herman, as "your grandmother." It was as though I had only one set of grandparents: my father's parents, who lived in a Brooklyn neighborhood not far from our old one. We saw them often. Very few details were handed down to me about my maternal grandmother, and what I knew seemed tragic.

On the final flight back to San Francisco I wondered: *Had the alarming history of madness begun when my grandmother was a new immigrant?*

1908–1913. Manhattan's Lower East Side

Morris and my grandmother, Yetta, who was from what is now Austria, met on a ship that took them to America in 1908. He was twenty-five and a woodturner. He told her he wanted to own a factory in a few years. Yetta, nineteen, said she would learn English and work in an office but would first be a seamstress in the factory where her distant cousin, Channa, worked, and everyone spoke Yiddish.

Both said they planned to save enough to bring family members to America. Each would stay with a relative on Manhattan's Lower East Side. Yetta would live with her cousin, who had two small children cared for by Channa's mother, "Bubbe,"[2] while Channa and her husband worked.

Morris and Yetta stood by the harbor a month later, watching ships coming and going. "You are beautiful," he said. "I think about you all the time." She blushed. She was in love with him too but wouldn't dare say so.

Later, they ate sandwiches at Katz's Delicatessen. By the time Morris walked her home, she knew they would marry.

Three months later, Yetta and Morris had a small Orthodox Jewish wedding in Channa's apartment, attended by the relatives they lived with and Gertie, a young woman Yetta befriended at the sewing factory.

Yetta wore Channa's wedding dress, a white, embroidered silk gown with lace and pearls. Once Gertie made a few alterations, it fit her perfectly, softly draping over her slim figure. Morris wore a fine wool gabardine suit. Yetta's eyes sparkled with love and excitement about beginning her new life. All through the ceremony, Morris looked only at her.

They moved into a flat a few blocks away, with a bedroom and combined kitchen and living area. Morris assured his bride, "We'll move into something grander uptown soon. I am progressing in my English classes. I will be promoted to journeyman and eventually to supervisor. It won't be long before we can bring family members to America."

Yetta nodded. She believed Morris; he sounded so sure. Yetta was too tired after working all day to concentrate on English classes at night. Almost everyone at the factory and in the neighborhood spoke Yiddish. Why struggle to learn a new language? She told Morris she would quit the class.

---

2   A glossary appears at the end of this book for definitions of Yiddish and Hebrew words and phrases.

"It doesn't matter," he said. "Soon, I will have my factory. We'll be on 'easy street,' and you won't need to work."

When Yetta's pregnancy began to show, she quit her job. She knew she'd get fired if she stayed longer, because others in the factory were let go once their condition became known.

Morris continued taking English classes. A woman in the class was also from Austria. Sometimes he stopped for a snack with her afterward. "It's nothing," he told Yetta. "We are like old friends." She looked sad and tried to believe him.

Their baby, Sadie, my Aunt "Sally," cried a lot at night during the first few months. Morris lost sleep and became too tired for English classes. He'd need to postpone his dream of a factory.

Now that Morris wasn't taking English classes, he had no excuse to see that woman, Yetta thought. Sadie settled down and began sleeping through the night. Morris liked being a father. He held Sadie on his lap, played peek-a-boo with her, and made up little songs. The family went on Sunday outings to the Bronx Zoo or Central Park and ferry rides to Staten Island.

Bubbe told Yetta that she would watch Sadie after she weaned her so she could return to work. Yetta hated leaving her baby but was grateful. Morris could barely support the family with what he earned. Now they would be able to save a little.

After two years of this arrangement, Bubbe started coughing. It was tuberculosis. Channa quit work to care for Bubbe and her children. Yetta had to leave her job to take care of Sadie. Soon, she was pregnant again.

"How can you do this to me? What a mess you've got me into," Morris said in bed before they went to sleep.

"I'm sorry," said Yetta. Though teary, she knew Morris had much to do with her pregnancy. She swallowed her tears and turned her back on him.

The next night he came home very late, drunk. He stormed in and slammed the door, waking Yetta.

"Oh, finally, you're home!" she called out, relieved, unaware of his state. "I was worried about you, afraid something hap—"

"It's too much," he shouted. "I can't handle it." He came close to where she sat up in bed. She smelled alcohol on his breath. More quietly, he said, "I'm too young for all this, never should have married, should have made something of myself first."

Yetta felt like he had stabbed her but said, "Oh, Morris, we'll get by. We have to be patient. I know it will be okay, because you are so good at what you do, and we'll figure something out and—"

"I cannot bear coming home to a pregnant wife and a child when I have nothing to give you, nothing to give myself—I can't even afford a new shirt. It all goes for rent and food, especially for milk for Sadie, and now in your condition, you need more milk too. And soon—another mouth to feed."

Yetta was crying, and Morris didn't seem to notice. He muttered, "I can't put up with this anymore."

He is going to leave me, Yetta thought. *If only Mama were here. I have no one to talk to. Channa is too busy taking care of Bubbe and her children. I feel like I'm imposing when I visit.*

Between her upset state and Morris's snoring, it took Yetta a while to fall asleep.

After Morris left for work the next day, Yetta watched Sadie napping in her crib. She felt calmer and more hopeful. *Maybe my mind is playing tricks on me. Perhaps he is just talking, letting out steam when he speaks that way, so much pressure building up in him like a steam engine. But where will his engine take him? Never mind! I must stay healthy and have a healthy baby.*

Yetta willed herself to be calm and patient with Morris, not to complain when he came home late, and not to respond when he needled her. She smiled, thinking Morris would love the new baby and things would be better again. *He will tell me I am a beautiful mother, like he used to do when Sadie was born.* She wrote to her mother that all was well. Why trouble her about nothing? *This* is *nothing, just a spell of bad weather.*

Morris paid little attention to Sadie, sometimes disappearing on Sundays instead of going to a park with his family. Even on the Sabbath, he was often not home for the candle lighting.

Sometimes, Morris worked on the Sabbath, saying he had to, or there would be no job.

"Shabbos! What does Shabbos have to do with us now? We're in America," he said.

Like many immigrants faithful to Jewish laws and customs in their "old country," Morris sometimes didn't wear a hat or yarmulke. He shaved his beard to avoid getting it caught in a machine at work, he said, but Yetta sensed it was his frenzy to become a "real American."

Maybe he's right, thought Yetta. *How will we get by if he refuses to work on the Sabbath and loses his job?* Still, she longed for the comfort of lighting candles to welcome the Sabbath with her husband. More often, though, she lit them with four-year-old Sadie asking, "Where's Papa?" while staring sadly at the flames.

Sadie stopped asking for her papa a couple of weeks after he disappeared, before the new baby arrived.

My mother, née Mollie Herman, was born at home at 192-½ Delancy Street. The father's name on her birth certificate stated "Morris Herman, address unknown." Channa arranged for the midwife and let Yetta live with her again, along with Sadie and Mollie.

Yetta hoped Morris would return. If only her mother were here. She thought, *Oh, Mama, I hoped to bring you here, have you close again. I wish I could put my head on your lap, have you hold me . . .*

Yetta wrote to her mother, describing the good parts of life in America with her children. Her mother sent small gifts for Sadie and Mollie. Yetta hadn't told her Morris was gone but sensed her mother knew. Channa must have written to her about that.

Mama is waiting for me to tell her myself, Yetta thought. *But how can I? It would make her worry. A new life I was supposed to have here. Some life! Well, I do have children.* She almost smiled. For a moment, she felt she had accomplished something grand in America. But when would Morris come back?

Before long, Yetta started acting strangely. She talked aloud to herself, obsessing about Morris. She wanted to believe his disappearance wasn't his fault, that he'd been taken away against his will or tricked into leaving. Did the woman he went for coffee with after English class force him into starting a new life with her? Yetta trembled at the thought: *had Morris gotten her pregnant?*

Yetta's mind raced with thoughts about Morris returning, picturing him smiling, saying her name over and over, hugging her as though he'd never let go. Then she imagined him on a big ship with sails. Was Morris drugged and shanghaied to work as part of a crew on a boat to China or elsewhere? Was he still alive? She woke up with sweat soaked through her nightgown.

Exhausted, Yetta became confused and forgot to eat. She asked strangers on the busy streets and familiar-looking pushcart vendors to help her find Morris. But what if he was on a ship? She went to the furniture factory where he used to work, but they knew nothing of him. Had he been abducted? Oh, Morris, poor Morris. Somehow, she would find him! People noticed her eyes' haunted quality, uncombed hair, and carelessly worn clothes.

Channa was at her wit's end, having her hands full caring for her own children and her sick mother, and now Yetta was falling apart. Channa and her husband felt helpless seeing her walk around their apartment dazed, forgetting to eat or to feed Sadie and her infant, Mollie. They heard Yetta cry at night and babble almost incomprehensibly, muttering things about Morris, a woman, and a ship.

They couldn't put Yetta and her children on the street; they needed shelter, food, and safety. But hadn't they done enough already for their distant relative? Eventually, they arranged for Yetta to be admitted to a local hospital. There, she continued babbling and showed no improvement. Yetta was then transferred to another facility. Eventually, she lived in Rockland State Hospital, a huge institution with several large, multi-story brick buildings in Orangeburg, New York. Many, including Yetta, stayed as inpatients for decades. For a long time she continued to think: *Morris will come for me soon. He loves me and our children. This is temporary.*

Sadly, my grandmother's situation was all too common. Like many disillusioned immigrants, my grandfather, Morris Herman, whom I never met, abandoned his wife and children in 1913. Many young men new to America married, fathered children, and deserted their families when their dreams of an easy life in the Golden Medina became a severe struggle to get by.

Safety nets didn't exist; families and *rebbes* who might have reminded these men to have faith and do the right thing were an ocean away. There were no public welfare programs to aid deserted mothers and children. Prosperous Jewish leaders in New York and other large cities raised private funds to build institutions to shelter Jewish children who were orphans and half-orphans, the term used for children with one remaining parent. The philanthropists' facilities were clean and well-managed, offering a safe alternative for children who otherwise might have been living on the streets or in Christian orphanages where they were at risk of being converted.

Yetta Herman's two girls—her infant, Mollie, and four-year-old Sadie—were taken to live in the Hebrew Orphan Asylum (H.O.A.) on 137th Street and Amsterdam Avenue. A vast, four-story brick building, it sheltered over a thousand children.

"No one wanted the burden of taking care of me," my mother told me, that night in my bedroom in 1956, adding, "I had no close relatives in America."

And Yetta? Much later, I learned that, as married adults, my mother and Aunt Sally, née Sadie, had wished their mother could live with one of them. But neither husband would allow it, which I imagine was heartbreaking. Yetta spent the rest of her life at Rockland State Hospital.

10 – Institutionalized

1974. Flight to San Francisco, California

A rawness lingered inside me, a disrupted sense of self that battled with the images of myself I treasured, of a young, attractive professional. As we approached our landing in San Francisco, thoughts of poor Yetta, poor Mom, poor all of us swirled like mists blurring past, present, and future.

1947. Rockland State Hospital, Orangeburg, NY

Gladys, a middle-aged attendant, sits in the day room of a ward for the chronically mentally ill at Rockland State Hospital in upstate New York. Wearing a pale-green uniform and hairnet, she sips coffee while keeping a desultory eye on the patients.

Most of them sit quietly on cracked vinyl chairs. Some stare vacantly at the beige walls; others have nodded off. One woman stands frozen in position with one arm bent behind her back, and the other stretched straight out, index finger pointing as though accusing—but aimed at no one. Another sits on the floor, facing a corner, with her arms crossed in front of her chest.

Gladys checks her watch. Both patients had remained as still as sculptures for over an hour. *Won't hurt to read the paper.* She picks up a tabloid on a table and smells ammonia.

"Hi, Gladys," says the janitress.

"Hi, Madge," she smiles.

Madge sets her mop and pail by the wall and pulls up a chair. She unwraps a piece of Wrigley's spearmint gum and hands a stick to Gladys. Her eyes are drawn to the photo on the newspaper's front page: Rita Hayworth in the arms of her costar and lover, Glenn Ford. "I'd give a million bucks for a guy like him," Madge says.

"You and me both. And I'd give a million to look like *her!*" Gladys cracks her gum, nodding.

Sensing someone nearby, Madge looks up and sees Yetta, now fifty-eight, in a faded housedress. More alert than most patients, Yetta helps out often enough to almost pass as a janitress without the uniform. Subdued by drugs, Yetta is too sluggish to match the tempo of a paid employee.

Over the years, Yetta's become overweight from the institution's food and lack of exercise. Her skin is pale from too little time outside. Her expression is bland from life's disappointments, lack of stimulation, or both.

"Hello, Yetta. How are you?" Madge asks.

Yetta doesn't answer; she still speaks no English. She looks towards the bucket and mop, brightening slightly, then stretches a stout arm toward it to signal, "Let me help. I want to mop. Okay?"

When she first came to this ward as a young woman, she tried to communicate verbally, but no one understood Yiddish. After a while, frustrated, she gave up and turned inward. She used to sit for long periods, one arm over the other on her lap, as though rocking a baby, actually two, because she seemed to alternate between a larger and smaller one. Sometimes she would cry, uttering in muffled tones: "Sadie . . . Mollie . . . Sadie . . . Mollie." Other times she would shout undecipherable words and scream something that sounded like "shanghaied," reaching out her arms as though to pull someone back.

When she was new here, Yetta often stood near the locked door, hoping to escape. Some attendants told a nurse on duty that this agitated patient was causing trouble. The nurse asked the doctor to prescribe something to calm her. He obliged, and the drug worked. Yetta, like many long-term patients here, takes the drug daily.

"Oh, you want to mop? Sure, go ahead." Madge smiles. "Good old Yetta," she says to Gladys. "I'd be exhausted if she didn't do half my job."

Yetta squishes the mop in the suds and goes to work, moving slowly, a side effect of the medicine. Yetta likes hearing her name spoken. She understands most of the English words but craftily does not let on. She's noticed that the staff stop talking when patients who understand English come near them, even if they're lost in their own worlds. Yetta craves the sound of human voices.

"She likes working," says Gladys. "It keeps her busy. I wish she could help me with *my* job. My back hurts from lifting the ones that refuse to move. The nurses call it *catatonia*. I call it *stubbornness*. My back calls it *evil*." She looks at the two, frozen-in-place patients.

"Well, maybe it's a sickness, and maybe it's not. If I were you, I'd poke 'em with a stick and see what moves and what don't." Madge stares at the statue-like woman with the accusing finger, then shakes her head.

Yetta winces; her back is to Madge and Gladys.

"Oh yeah, I do that, and the supervisor will be after me. I call her the *snoopervisor*; she sees me, and before you can say *boo*, I'm out on the street. I'm too sane to get free room and board like them," Gladys says, eyeing one stiff body, then the other, "and too tired to find another job. Anyway, they probably can't help it," she says, her tone changing to compassionate. Feeling guilty, she adds, "It's my aching back, not me, talking."

Yetta moves away, her face a void, mop in hand. She has heard enough.

Gladys glances at Yetta's back. "Now that one, such a shame. She's been here as long as me, over twenty years. They'd let her go home if she had somewhere to go and someone to take care of her. She's got two daughters who visit now and then, but they live far away. One of 'em came last week. She says she wants to take her, but her husband don't. Same thing with the other daughter: the husband says no."

Aunt Sally with Yetta
at the Rockland State Hospital.

"Tsk, tsk." The janitress returns her attention to the tabloid.

"You should'a seen her when she first came. A real beauty. Except for how sad she looked. Confused too. Had these screaming fits. Now she's so used to it here, and she don't look so sad no more and even smiles sometimes. Maybe it's just as well she stays here."

"Mm," the janitress nods absently, eyes riveted to an inside photo of Rita Hayworth cavorting with her lover.

"She's got grandchildren she's never seen, though," Gladys says pensively, more to herself, as her coworker looks absorbed.

"Her daughters won't bring 'em. Say they don't want to upset 'em." She shakes her head. "It's too bad, but maybe for the best."

Yetta is too far away to hear her. Her bland face takes on a crafty little smile as she paints a wet circle on the floor surrounding the standing statue. Head bent towards the linoleum she cleans, Yetta's straight, graying hair flops forward, hiding her mouth until she straightens her neck and resumes an emotionless expression. She aims the mop towards the frozen man facing a corner, and then glides the mop in a circle around him.

Yetta stops cleaning, closes her eyes, and intones in Yiddish, "Morris, where are you? How can you disappear?" She lifts the mop automatically and is about to scrub more of the floor but stops. Her face contorts in pain. "Babies!" She releases the mop, its stick making a *clunk* sound on the floor. She closes her eyes and covers her face with her hands. "My babies! I want my babies," she screams, then collapses in a heap, sobbing.

11 – Vulnerable

1974. San Francisco, California

When I returned to work, Harry looked glad to see me. He wasn't one to show emotion, but his lips smiled, and his eyes were soft. He gestured for me to sit in the chair by his desk and waited for me to speak.

"Harry, you have been wonderful. Your support on the phone made me feel so good."

He smiled nervously and nodded. "Take it easy for a few days. You've been through a lot. You don't need to schedule sessions with your patients right away."

What a guy! Handsome too. Three years my senior, he's tall and well-built. Dark brown hair, a trim beard, searching eyes. I'd had a little crush on him before I knew he had a girlfriend, a pretty social worker, whom he'd recently married. They met at a professional training event where participants were encouraged to bare their souls.

"I'm fine now."

But he looked at me in that psychologist-searching way, as though to say, *You might as well tell me everything; I can see through you.*

"I'm much better now that I'm back. I've had some amazing insights and experiences that will help my work, like what happens to some people on acid." I'd seen Harry high on marijuana at enough parties that I assumed he'd tripped on LSD.

"Um," he murmured, which could have meant either "Let's not get into that" or "I don't know what to make of you."

"It was an ordeal, but it's over, and I'm so-o-o glad to be here and ready to work."

Being ready to work could mean different things in this setting, and I was beginning to feel spacey; my eyes weren't focusing well. Was it the Prolixin?

"Well, you've been through a lot," Harry repeated. "Take care of yourself." As I left, he put his hand on my shoulder, meaning, "Hang in there."

I took this advice to heart. I knew I might face some awkward transitions ahead. I was embarrassed to face Alan during my first therapy session after my New York ordeal. I acknowledged my mistake in thinking we'd have a romantic relationship.

Alan said, "It's not unusual for therapy clients to fantasize about having an intimate relationship with their therapist because of the transference that develops."

Of course, I knew this intellectually. As a therapist, I'd been on the receiving end of such fantasies, but it had never been delusional. During subsequent sessions, I talked about work. I had a light caseload of patients I'd seen for a while, and that was going well.

But my relationships with some of my colleagues shifted. Most of them were also in therapy, and many continued as patients in the after-hours group led by Alfred. No one seemed to mind the complications of Alfred's dual relationship—which professional ethics codes prohibited—serving as both the supervisor of clinical staff and their therapist. Steve, Doreen, and others were in the group, but I wasn't; for me, it crossed too many boundaries.

Seeing a therapist as an outpatient was admirable in our agency's culture. Investing time and money to gain self-understanding helped us stay objective and made it less likely that we would project our values or emotions onto our clients. Our therapy helped us gain tools for dealing with countertransference when our personal leanings could get in the way of practicing professional therapy.

"I'm dealing with it in therapy" had been an acceptable excuse, no matter how unethically or outrageously a therapist at our agency behaved. I'd heard that Steve had had sex with a female inpatient in the agency's rehabilitation program before I started to work there. If this unethical behavior had happened elsewhere, I imagine the perpetrator would have lost his job and reputation. Steve kept both after saying, "I'm dealing with it in therapy."

But, apparently, what I did was unforgivable. After welcoming me back, some colleagues began to cool off and distance themselves. By crossing the line that separated neurotic, everyday folks from psychotics, I'd joined the ranks of the "untouchables." The label, "inpatient psychiatric patient," might as well have been embroidered on my clothes like Hester Prynne's scarlet letter. I sensed that those who avoided me feared subconsciously that if it happened to me, it could happen to them; in the blink of an eye, they too could lose touch with reality. Formerly respectful colleagues began looking for signs that I was still crazy.

It hadn't helped that in my euphoria to be back at work, I let my new, trust-my-gut self come out, like when I crocheted at a staff meeting. Some experienced therapists I'd encountered during my internship year in Detroit, had crocheted or knit during staff meetings. So I thought, *Why not calm my mind by crocheting?* I tried to ignore some stares and covert glances and Alfred's raised eyebrows.

These people are small-minded and rigid. What's wrong with crocheting? They should get used to it.

A couple of days later, at a staff training event in the solarium, Carla, the consultant who led the anger workshop, asked us to state an imagined identity for ourselves and act it out in a short role-play.

"A housewife with two children," I said, shocking myself when it was my turn. Steve and Doreen stared at me, also surprised. Wasn't I the happily unencumbered, stylish single woman?

Although I'd embraced the idea of women's liberation, I interpreted it differently from some of its banner carriers. I would not become enslaved by the tyranny of women's liberation. I still liked it when men held doors open for me and paid for dinner dates. Yet, I became a follower of the feminist party line in many ways. I wanted equal rights to do whatever was in vogue, from moving up the ladder of success at work to romantic involvement with anyone who struck my fancy. I rarely, if ever, talked about having children.

Our role-play began innocently enough. Steve offered to play my young son, and Vicki played my daughter. The three of us sat on the floor while being observed by the circle of staff members surrounding us.

Suddenly, Steve's mouth grazed my blouse, and he pretended to breastfeed, making loud sucking noises.

My face burned. A jumble of emotions confounded me. I tried to swat Steve away, but he ducked out of reach with a goofy grin. No one in the circle around us made a sound. Vicki, caught off guard, looked away.

My eyes shot darts at Steve while he smiled lewdly.

Was I supposed to be a good sport? I returned to my chair in the circle, feeling shame and rage.

Sickening, I thought later, about Steve's violation and everyone's silence. No one defended me or expressed sympathy. I later wondered whether their lack of response was a sign of the group's dysfunctionality or if all were simply caught off-guard by Steve's grossness.

In the office we shared with Doreen, Steve had revealed way more of his *mishegoss* than I cared to know, including his sexual impotence when I first started working at the agency. Yet, after I returned from New York, he refused to meet my eyes at a staff meeting and generally avoided me or stole an occasional nervous glance my way. But what he did today was disgusting.

Steve could talk till the cows came home about his sexual failures and perverse fantasies and even get away with having sex with a patient, with no repercussions. And now this! Because I was labeled "mentally ill," he thought he could get away with assaulting my body.

It seemed he could. I'd been a sitting duck; I could have worn a "kick-me" sign.

Back then, I had little energy to confront people who violated my boundaries. I often failed to recognize such intrusions, other than feeling a vague sense of discomfort. A classic example was when Don, a psychiatrist who supervised some of my clinical work, said, "You're jealous of your sister." His job was to discuss my cases with me. Now that I was sad and vulnerable, he intruded into my personal life. Besides, he was wrong. I was happy for Gloria.

But I became mute and didn't know how to reply.

"Have an affair," Don continued. "Get it out physically. Wrestle with someone, maybe Stuart. Yes, you should ask him to wrestle with you." Stuart, the handsome rehabilitation counselor who had left his wife and young children to marry his current wife. Don was way off with both ideas, but then he crossed a more serious line.

Don and I habitually ended our weekly supervision sessions with a chaste hug. But this day, he squeezed my breasts as we released from an embrace. I looked at him, stunned. He shrugged his shoulders as though nothing had happened—I felt like it was open season on me.

When I told Alan about this in therapy, he said to tell Don that what he did was unacceptable and that I didn't want it to happen again.

When I said that to Don, he said, "It's theater," but it didn't happen again.

12 – Amy's Wedding

I regained my colleagues' respect as time passed. I saw clients, provided clinical supervision to several staff members, and coordinated the agency's internship program.

At a staff meeting, Harry announced a call for papers to present at a national conference on alcoholism and other drug problems in San Francisco. I wrote "Homeostasis: A Key Concept in Working with Alcoholic Family Systems." I was grateful to Carla for encouraging me and suggesting the title.

My article included case examples of two families with alcoholic fathers. I was excited about writing my first professional paper. When I felt challenged midway, I dropped my head on my desk, overwhelmed and tempted to give up. "Write the paper!" Doreen commanded like a drill sergeant from her corner of our office. Thanks to her, I pushed on, finished it, and was thrilled when it was accepted for presentation at the conference.

This was an expansive time in other ways too. I spent most weekends at the ski cabin a group of us rented. I took a solo trip in my 1969 Volvo to Utah's Snowbird ski resort. During a blizzard on the way, I put on tire chains and kept driving. I skied daily for a week on fabulous white powder, soaked in a hot tub, rolled in the snow on a dare, and socialized at night with friendly people.

The drive through vast open spaces exhilarated me. My mind drifted where it wanted. I felt pure joy—strong, free, and happy—driving ninety miles an hour in Utah and Nevada, with no one caring because mine was the only car in sight.

Back home, I told Alan I was ready to stop therapy. He was silent.

"Do you think I'm ready to stop?" I asked, seated across the desk from him.

"It's your decision."

"Yes, I know, but I want you to agree."

I tried to read Alan's eyes for a sign. His glasses slipped down on his nose; his face showed no expression.

"You look as though you weren't expecting me to stop." Again, I looked for clues. Was he a blank screen on which I projected and attributed my feelings to him? Or was he really feeling something, and I didn't mean romantically? That was out of the question since he'd set me straight on the phone while I was at Booth Memorial. Was he feeling anxious? That's what I read on his face. But was it his anxiety about ending therapy or mine?

"Tell me more," he said. "What are you thinking about this minute?"

I felt ready to move on. Wasn't therapy about learning to trust myself?

"Therapy has been wonderful for me. I don't know what I would have done without it. I'm much more aware of my feelings now."

Alan opened his mouth to speak, then closed it. He pushed his glasses back to the bridge of his nose and stared at me, seeming to grope for the right words. He took a deep breath.

"Yes, you have done some good work here," he said. "There *is* one area we haven't dealt with, though."

What could he mean? I'd told things I couldn't have said to anyone else. What was left to talk about?

"We haven't talked about hostility."

Hostility? I drew a blank. Why bring that up now? I'd gotten out my anger, hadn't I? At the anger workshop, the chair I'd smashed represented my father. Certainly, I'd lashed out at my mother, although I didn't want to think about her.

"I don't know what you mean. I think I'm doing fine. I'm trusting myself much more, and I want to trust my feeling that I'm ready to stop coming here."

Alan nodded solemnly as though accepting my decision.

This was our final session. It felt like ending a chapter. I was relieved to free myself from these scheduled appointments and felt confident and independent.

By then, I'd nearly forgotten my delusion that Alan was in love with me and wanted to marry me. My mind had been playing tricks on me.

Meanwhile, Amy had good news. "Michael and I are engaged," she wrote. "You are my oldest and dearest friend, and I want you to be my maid of honor." Amy had written earlier about long walks with Michael and conversations that hinted at a future together.

Three months later, I flew to New York for the wedding and stayed at Gloria and Larry's house in Pomona, Rockland County, where I was excited to meet their first child, my three-month-old niece, Rachel.

Still estranged from my mother, I asked everyone to keep my visit a secret from her. I feared seeing her would set me off and land me in Elmhurst again. I wouldn't feel safe until I returned to California on schedule.

Everything went well in New York this time. I slept and ate well at Gloria's house. I loved being an aunt and that Gloria trusted me to babysit for Rachel. The last time I'd seen my sister was when she and Larry visited me at Booth Memorial a year earlier, and she'd seemed unfazed about my having missed her wedding.

My niece was adorable and felt lovely in my arms. "We are going to be good friends, Rachel," I said, giving her a bottle from which she eagerly sucked.

Unlike Gloria, who always wanted children, I rarely thought about motherhood. I hoped for it someday, but abstractly, rather than as a yearning.

Just before Amy and Michael's Sunday afternoon ceremony, I met Michael, a college engineering teacher, for the first time in the restaurant where the wedding would be. Like the couple about to wed, it was tasteful and unpretentious. I felt warmed by Michael's sensitive face and sweet smile. In contrast to Amy's soft, full figure, Michael was slim and wiry. He practiced karate daily. His eyes, behind wire-framed glasses, lit up often, especially when he looked at Amy.

Amy had sent me a sketch of her dress. Now, we looked like we shopped together rather than on opposite sides of the continent. She wore a long voile dress with a floral pattern in muted pastel tones over a pale, cream background. My dress was a similar style and material, with deeper-colored pastel flowers. We both wore straw hats with wide brims similar to those of women outdoors in French Impressionistic paintings. During the ceremony, Amy and I carried bouquets of roses and carnations.

The young rabbi performing the ceremony changed the part where the couple pledges to be faithful, saying, "Amy and Michael will decide whatever being faithful means to them."

An Age-of-Aquarius rabbi. When did faithfulness become negotiable?

I sat with Amy and Michael during the luncheon. Their faces glowed. "I'm very happy for both of you," I told Michael. "But I'm also jealous. I'm losing Amy."

"No, you still have her, and you're gaining me," he said, eyes twinkling, and I believed him.

Flying home to California, I was relieved that my fear of getting locked up again in New York was irrational. I made it! I hadn't gone crazy—whatever that meant. I still suspected that the fault for my hospitalizations lay with others. I remembered how alive I had felt, connected to everyone, and insightful. Yet they locked me up. The whole episode had been a fluke; my treatment was brutal.

My plane touched down in San Francisco. *Home, at last.*

13 – Attempted Seduction

1975. Berkeley, California

In my apartment that night, I didn't sleep. My mind kept racing. Once again I imagined Alan and me together forever. When I first met him in his office, I was weak and frightened. *Now I know myself well, thanks to him, and we'll spend the rest of our lives together.*

Tossing in my waterbed, hugging my Red Riding Hood doll, I remembered Alan's words when I phoned him from Booth Memorial a year ago: "I have no intention of marrying you."

No intention. What had that meant, anyway? Was it just how he felt at the moment? What ethical therapist would *intend* to get involved with his patient? He was saying what a therapist had to say, fighting the feelings I knew were inside him.

But now I'm not his patient! I quit therapy over three months ago. He has done a great job concealing his love all this time, but I know . . . Still, I couldn't escape wondering if maybe I was wrong. *Could all this be my imagination? No. I cannot think that way. I'm sure he loves me. But what if he doesn't?*

I shifted back and forth all night in a mental version of the daisy game: he loves me; he loves me not; he loves me; he loves me not; he loves me . . .

I had to settle this once and for all.

The next morning, trembling all over: my arms, shoulders, legs, every part of me. *Stop it!* But my body wouldn't listen. I drew Red Riding Hood into a long hug, then put her down, calmer. I took a few deep breaths, sat on my waterbed's frame, phoned Alan's work number, and learned he no longer worked there.

When I phoned his home number in Berkeley, I was relieved to hear his hello. Same soft, deep voice.

"Alan, I need to see you." My voice was unsteady.

"I'm not working as a therapist anymore."

Maybe that's just as well; no problem with professional ethics.

"You sound shaky. Are you all right?"

"I don't know. I can't go to work today. I didn't sleep well last night. My thoughts are racing. I'm scared. Can I come to see you?"

After a pause, he said, "Okay."

He loves me.

He gave driving directions.

Too busy to think about eating, I grabbed a few things for the trip across the San Francisco Bay Bridge to Alan's Berkeley apartment. On the passenger seat of my Volvo, I set a spare pair of underpants, a nightgown, and my Red Riding Hood doll. Beside me in the car, she felt like my alter ego, a good friend to help steady my nerves.

It seemed unbelievable yet inevitable that I was finally going to Alan's home. It sat on a quiet, tree-lined street. The late after-noon sun warmed me and brightened the flowers in front of his place.

I could live here. I climbed the stairs to his flat.

When he opened the door, I saw the same Alan. His hair flopped over his ears, and he wore a short-sleeved, button-down shirt and Levis. His sweet face bore a shy, questioning look and his usual trace of acne, which I found boyishly endearing on him.

He gestured me into his living room, where he sat on an easy chair, and I settled on the couch opposite him. "What's going on?" he asked, more composed now, watching me intently, as a therapist might. Or a concerned friend.

"I'm not sleeping. I'm jumpy and scared."

"You're not my client anymore. I want to help, but—"

"I'm so glad you let me come. I feel better just being near you."

"Well, er—"

"Oh, no. Am I making you nervous?" *You do love me. But you're afraid to say it.* "I'll try to slow down." I took a few deep breaths. He stared at me. I wondered what he was thinking.

"Alan, I understand. You can't say it, so I will. I think you have feelings for me, and it's hard. You think maybe it's not okay because you were my therapist." *Why is he staring at me like a clinician, nudging his glasses higher on his nose, just like he used to in our sessions?* His apparent detachment unnerved me.

"Marcia, I'm not sure you understand. There is nothing like that between us—"

"Oh, you're still pretending. I know what I know, and I don't plan to leave until you tell me you know too."

"You are mistaken."

"Alan, you're the mistaken one. You don't know your true feelings for me."

"Do you want to be carted off to a mental hospital again?"

He might as well have stabbed me with a butcher's knife.

"How dare you?" I said, enraged. Was he threatening me? "There is nothing wrong with me. It's *you* who has a problem. You can't face it. We are so right together."

Alan didn't get me carted off to a mental hospital. He let me hang around for several hours and offered me food. I accepted an orange and sensed it was a gift of love. Not hungry, I refused a sandwich and agreed to a cup of tea.

It was late when I decided to seduce him, unbuttoning my blouse slowly until it was open enough for my bra to peek through. *He cannot take his eyes off me.* As I began removing my blouse, his lips widened into a smile. Then he looked down at his knees and fidgeted with his fingers. *I know he's turned on. Finally, something's about to happen!*

He clasped his hands. When he looked up, his mouth was in a straight line. "No, no, no. Put it back on." His voice was firm.

I rebuttoned my blouse, humiliated. We'd both said it all. I grabbed my purse and rushed out the door.

Entering my car, I saw my underwear and nightgown on the passenger seat. The doll comforted me, but I felt alone.

I drove back to dark, deserted University Avenue, which felt eerie after midnight, with all its shops closed.

I needed a telephone. I found a pay phone booth in a closed gas station. Giving no thought to possible danger, or the fact that I'd estranged myself from her for a year, or that it was after three a.m. in Rockaway, I phoned my mother.

14 – Reconciliation

1975. Berkeley, California

My mother answered on the first ring with a groggy, muffled hello.

"Did I wake you?"

"That's okay, sweetie. How are you, Marcia?" she asked, sounding more alert. Her tone suggested she wasn't surprised to hear from me or at this hour. "Are you okay?"

"I'm fine, Mom. I feel fine, but I had a rough time today."

"Oh, no!" My mother tended to respond to a hint of disappointment from me as if I'd been severely injured physically or lost everything in an earthquake. I was exasperated, yet reassured. Suddenly, my trouble felt inconsequential. I was still alive, all physical parts and possessions intact.

I barely noticed an occasional car moving along University Avenue as we spoke. The phone booth was dimly lit; the world had disappeared; it was just my mother and me. The night was a womb.

"There's this guy, but it's not working out."

"Oh, Marcia!"

"It's okay; a misunderstanding. He's a good person; he doesn't feel the way about me I thought he did. Now I know." I could have been speaking to a best friend. I was relieved to talk to my mother again and feel her love and support. I understood that I'd always loved her. Our bond was deeper than I could have imagined. It felt like we spoke every day.

"Forget about him. These things happen. Don't give it a second thought. Save your energy for something good. It will come. You've always been popular." She paused briefly, then said quickly, as though remembering something important. "I am so glad you called. I wanted to tell you something. I'm going to send you a check."

"A check?"

"Yes, for two thousand."

"That's nice, Mom, but what for?" Sometimes, instead of a nightgown or sweater, she'd sent me twenty-five or fifty dollars for my birthday, but that was three months away.

"That's what I gave Gloria when she got married. I believe in women's liberation. So you should get the same thing, married or single."

I smiled grimly at her logic. *My mother is a trip. Women's lib!* Here she was, intuitively picking up the pieces of my broken self, showing she was there for me in her zany way.

"Thanks, Mom," I laughed. "I love you."

"Don't tell your sister."

There she goes again. She's always tried to be even with Gloria and me. "Are you afraid Gloria will be jealous if she finds out I got the same money for nothing?"

My mother was silent.

I sighed, burdened with the secret. As likely as not, she'd let it slip to Gloria, and I'd get the fallout.

Still, I was thrilled that she'd been thinking of me and wanting to give to me, even though I had cut her off for so long. During the few minutes we talked, I felt safe, as buoyant as though I'd grabbed a lifeline in a troubled sea.

15 – Gifts for Colleagues

1975. San Francisco, California

After talking to my mother, I drove over the San Francisco Bay Bridge feeling disconnected from time and space. I was heading south toward the Sunset District of San Francisco, past the turnoff to go home.

My mind was as foggy as the air, but I switched my course, going north toward the Golden Gate Bridge in a thick mist. I could barely see and hardly cared where I was, yet I ended up in the Marina district and parked near my apartment.

I plopped on my waterbed in my dark room, but my mind was too busy to sleep. I turned on a lamp and stared at a poster that had intrigued me at a small North Beach shop. It was a simple black print on white paper, framed in shiny, black wood. I focused on the sketched figures: an old Jewish teacher with a beard and yarmulke wearing a garment with fringes hanging below his waist. He's instructing a similarly attired young boy. The words were near the teacher's head: "When we write the name of G-d, the two yuds must be on the same level. They must stand side by side as equals. When one is above the other, the name of G-d is not."

Harry must have this, I thought, ignoring that he wasn't Jewish. *He treats us all as equals. Harry's the perfect boss, always so caring and understanding. Like when he had said, "You're having growing pains."*

Growing pains. What a supportive way to view my struggles. Side by side, as equals, we worked together, even though he was the boss. Perfect, perfect, perfect. Carefully, I lifted the poster off the wall, touching only its frame, and put it in a large shopping bag.

Next, the pillow I made at Booth Memorial caught my eye. Its wool was still crisp and new-looking, and the three broad stripes of russet, dark-green, and taupe were striking. *Perfect for Doreen. Sometimes she treats me like a rival; she was the young, pretty staff member until I came along. She worried about me when I was at Elmhurst. Underneath all the ups and downs, I know she cares. Doreen is like a sister.*

I put the pillow in the shopping bag and tossed in a few more treasures for others. My mind raced through dawn. I could hardly wait to get to the office. Everyone there had helped me grow. *Growing pains.* Harry was right about that. Sometimes, it was painful, sloshing through self-doubts, but now I felt joyous. *No failures, only lessons. I will give back. My clients, too, will gain so much from me because of my special powers to help them heal.*

Before I knew it, it was daylight. I forgot to eat and didn't change my clothes or comb my hair. When I drove to work, my doll, nightgown, and underpants were still in the passenger seat.

Doreen was already there. She stared at me wide-eyed.

"Marcia, what *happened* to you?"

"What do you mean? I'm fine. I've just been busy. Here! For you," I said, grabbing the pillow from the bag and thrusting it at her.

She took it, hesitating slightly. "Er . . . thanks." She watched me guardedly as though searching for a clue. "But are you sure you're okay? You look like—maybe you need to rest."

"Don't be silly. I'm fine," I snapped. "Is Harry around? I need to see him right away."

"Better wait. He's leading the group for recently discharged inpatients."

Wait? I don't know what wait *means.* I seized the framed poster and charged down the hall, opening some doors without knocking, banging on others first, before rushing in without waiting for a response.

Must find Harry.

I barged in on Dick Jones, the psychiatrist with whom I co-led an art therapy group. He was holding an individual therapy session. When he saw me, his mouth dropped open. I didn't know why he looked so surprised, but I rushed back out to find Harry. As I opened and quickly slammed each door on not seeing him, I ignored the startled expressions.

Finally, I opened the right door, hurried through the circle of recently discharged inpatients, and dropped the poster in Harry's lap. He gulped and said, "Uh . . ."

I banged the door shut as I left the room.

When I rushed toward the secretary's office, Dick Jones opened the door of his interviewing room. "Are you okay, Marcia?"

I stopped, looked at him, and ran down the hall, shouting, "I'M FINE! I'VE NEVER BEEN BETTER. ARE YOU OKAY?"

"I'm worried about you, Marcia. I want to talk to you in a few minutes when my session's over," Dick called after me.

"GOOD, BECAUSE I'M WORRIED ABOUT YOU TOO," I yelled before ducking into the large office where two secretaries worked and the patients' charts were filed. I removed the file of a client scheduled to see me that morning, put it on a table, and pulled up a chair. I tried futilely to review my notes from last week's session but found it too hard to focus. *So much to think about. More gifts to give my dear coworkers. Better find my shopping bag.*

I closed the chart and was about to leave the room when Dick came and sat by me; just the two of us were present.

"Marcia, it's not like you to barge in during a therapy session. Something's wrong. I want to help."

"Dick, you are wonderful, and I want to help you." I looked into his pale-blue eyes and took in his delicate features, stringy, brown, shoulder-length hair, and droopy mustache. He held my gaze and spoke softly in his southern accent. "I don't tell many people about this, but when I was in the army long ago, I became psychotic and was hospitalized. So I may be able to help if you can talk to me about what's going—"

"Here's how I can help you," I interrupted. "You act like you're gay. But I know you're pretending. You like women." I hopped into Dick's lap and put my arms around his neck. His face turned beet red. He shook his head but smiled, embarrassed, I gathered, because he knew I was on to him.

"Maybe you can draw your mixed-up feelings about women during one of our art therapy groups," I said. "You know how grateful I am to you for training me to do art therapy and choosing me be your co-therapist. Now, I want to help you."

I read fear in his eyes.

"Don't be afraid. It will be good," I said gently, giving his shoulder a playful squeeze.

A secretary, Nan, entered the room, did a double-take, and quickly recovered. "Marcia, your patient is here." She sat at her desk and focused on paperwork.

I rose from Dick's lap. "We'll continue later," I said with a parting wink.

I greeted my patient in the hall, a slim, depressed, shaggy-haired young man prone to existential discussions. I reverted to automatic pilot as we walked into an interviewing room. After we sat, I said, "I'm feeling spacey today."

He met my eyes and nodded like it was no problem. "I want to show you something I wrote," he said. He removed a thin, white sheet of onionskin from his pocket, folded in quarters, and handed it to me. I opened it and silently read the typed words:

> *satori*
> *I am but*
> *a puzzle piece*

I realized
while pissing
then realized
that without me
there would be
one piece missing

Wow! Amazing. My eyes moistened. I felt deeply connected to him, as though we possessed the same soul. I was sure he felt this, too. *His poem is my poem; our energies have merged.* I regarded him beatifically and spewed out some metaphysical ramblings. He appeared to take it all in, accepting me.

I felt tired and wanted to sink my head onto the desk. But as I started to, I remembered he was my patient, so I sat up and feigned attentiveness.

"Take care of yourself," he said on his way out.

He knows I'm out of it and doesn't mind.

I smiled a relieved goodbye.

I went back to the secretary's office to hang out. *How will I get through this day?* I put my head on a vacant desk. As I let out a loud sigh, the secretary, Nan, tried to catch my attention.

"Ahem," she cleared her throat.

I saw Mr. and Mrs. B. poking their heads into the doorway from the hall. *Oh! What are they doing here?* They regarded me expectantly. It clicked that they were waiting for me to usher them down to the room where I'd seen them for weekly couples therapy for the past year. *Of course, they're here.*

I looked at them, aghast. There was no way I could have coped with another session that day. My head was spinning, and I had no idea what to do about them. I didn't want to talk to *anybody*. Not even to these two, who felt almost like family in the best sense. They depended on me, but I couldn't do it.

I shook my head. "I'm sorry. Just can't."

"It's okay," said Mr. B. I read compassion on both faces before they turned to leave.

My buddy, the head nurse, June, came in with Dick, who waited near the door. June approached me. *Why do they both look so sad? As if someone died.*

June looked into my eyes. When she smiled, as she did then, her pretty, round face lit up. "Marcia, do you trust me?"

I gazed at her smooth, rosy complexion and briefly at the rest of her. She was as obese as ever and, as always, stylishly dressed. A big, beautiful mama. She had always been my staunchest supporter at work. Of course, I trusted her. I nodded almost imperceptibly and smiled, yet I sensed danger.

"Let's go for a ride," she said.

16 – Langley Porter Psychiatric Hospital

1975. San Francisco, California

Dick rode shotgun in June's Buick. Squeezed in the back between Vicki and Willie, a psych tech who was Doreen's new boyfriend, I felt I was among friends.

"Where are we going?"

"I'm taking you to see a doctor," June said. She parked near Mount Zion Hospital, where we all went inside. An employee ushered me into a room where a man in a white lab coat filled out some forms.

I must have been given a powerful tranquilizer because, the next thing I knew, I'd woken up across town at Langley Porter Psychiatric Hospital.

As a child welfare worker, my first professional job, I'd been at Langley Porter for case conferences with the pleasant young psychiatrist of an autistic girl on my foster placement caseload. We used to meet in his office off the children's ward.

The ward I was locked in looked like a large, L-shaped living room with couches, chairs, coffee tables, a ping-pong table, and a large bin with arts and crafts supplies. Inside it, I saw yarn and knitting needles, among other supplies. The room's walls were in pale, pastel tones; the furnishings were clean and in good condition. Patients wore their own clothes and seemed mentally clear.

Willie visited the next day. I gave him my apartment key and a list of clothes and toiletries, which he brought. My friend and ski buddy Mimi stopped by with flowers. Coworkers phoned and gave me cards. All this felt good, yet I was shocked to be there.

The tranquilizer they injected at Mt. Zion had done its job. Enough of it had left my system for me to feel more like myself. I wanted to work, see friends, and get my life back.

I played ping-pong with Henry, a stocky, lively patient around my age. He cracked jokes as he slammed back my shots. The score was close to even.

"Hey, where'd you learn to play so well?" he asked.

"My father taught me when I was a kid." I pictured how Dad's eyes would light up when I surprised him with a good slam or shot back one of his.

Henry sent a high one my way, and I smashed it back. His mouth dropped open when the ball grazed the table's edge and landed at his feet.

"Hey, I could learn some tricks from you," he said.

"Just lucky." I was having so much fun I almost forgot where I was.

"This your first time here?"

"Yeah, but I was at another place last year. It was awful. Langley Porter's a palace compared with that snake pit." My stomach tightened at the thought of Elmhurst; then I relaxed again in the game's rhythm.

He nodded. "I've been in worse too. This place is one of the better ones. It's like—smaller, more personal. Nicer atmosphere, if you know what I mean."

"Hey, you could write a tourist guidebook for the mentally ill and compare the facilities." We both laughed. I continued, "You could rate them, give them a different number of stars or diamonds for service, appearance, etcetera."

"Yeah, I could compare the doctors, the food, the furniture, the buildings—"

"The patients, visiting policies, bathrooms," I added. He laughed louder.

"Ha, ha! Hey, you crack me up. What did you say your name was?"

"Marcia." I surprised him with a slam, but he lobbed it back. He caught me off-guard, I missed, and he won the game.

Later, I took yarn from the bin and started knitting a pillow cover in earth tones, like those of the pillow I'd given to Doreen during my recent manic spree at work. Feeling the wool against my skin and the repetitive clicking of the knitting needles soothed me. I looked forward to finishing the pillow and sleeping with it at home soon.

I relaxed on a couch near a teenage girl with a soft, pretty face and shoulder-length, well-groomed hair. While continuing to knit, I asked her why she was there.

"Anorexia nervosa," she said, surprising me. I'd heard about young women who starved themselves to emaciation and worse, but until then, I'd never met one.

Conversation flowed easily between patients. No one seemed too heavily medicated, and we all had time. It felt like a comfortable dormitory, but I'd rather have been home. Whatever happened to me that got me there seemed over.

On my third day at Langley Porter, a thin, balding psychologist with wire-rimmed glasses, gave me the MMPI exam, the Minnesota Multiphasic Personality Inventory. After scoring it, he brought me into his office, which had a glass wall that looked into the hallway.

He said, "When you were at Mt. Zion, you said Alan Tobin was your therapist. But when I spoke with him, he said he no longer is. He said he does not want to be involved."

He loves me, not. Alan had left no room for doubt. I experienced a cold feeling of finality.

"I've also talked to some people where you work. You are respected there as a serious professional with high standards, sometimes perfectionistic. This makes it very important that you take what I recommend seriously. Your career is at stake. The MMPI indicates that you have *manic-depressive illness*."[3]

What? That was impossible. He was being dramatic about my career. Two nights without sleeping and then that long, miserable ordeal with Alan. Stressful, yes, but not *pathological*.

"It is important that you begin taking lithium immediately, a very effective drug for this condition."

I shook my head. "No, I don't think so." *My coworkers think I'm perfectionistic? What did they mean by that?* This was ridiculous. He wasn't talking about me. I'd just been under a lot of pressure, traveling to New York, the intensity of Amy's wedding, seeing Gloria, Larry, my new baby niece, not seeing my mother, and Alan's rejection.

"Here," the psychologist said, showing me the test result plotted on a graph. A line ascended higher and higher across the chart, but what did it prove? "This is the classic profile for manic-depressive illness."

I'd never believed much in psychological testing; it seemed like a lot of gobbledy-gook.

"If you do not take lithium, you will destroy your professional career," he said.

What did *he* know? I didn't need medicine.

"Think it over while you're here."

"How long do I need to be here?"

"Your three-day hold ends today. We would like you to sign a voluntary admission form so we can continue to treat you and make sure you are stable before leaving."

"But I feel fine. I want to go home."

---

3 The term "manic-depressive illness" has been replaced with "bipolar disorder" since the 1980 release of the *Diagnostic and Statistical Manual of Mental Disorders* (DSM-III).

"As a voluntary patient, you can be discharged at any time. But I suggest you stay until we feel ready for you to leave and have a stable lithium level. Meanwhile, you can get a pass to go to your apartment. If you leave before we think you're ready, you will be discharged 'AMA,' against medical advice."

"I don't want the medicine. I feel fine and want to leave as soon as possible. But I'll stay a little longer if I can get a pass. My car's in the parking lot where I work. I want to get it, drive to my apartment, check my phone messages and mail."

Willie came by that Friday to drive me to my car. Inside it, I saw Red Riding Hood, my nightgown, and underpants on the passenger seat. All this time, they'd been in plain sight for the people I worked with to see. *Oh, well, too late now.*

The phone in my apartment rang. It was Len Epstein, whom I'd met briefly at a party two weeks ago. "Yes, I remember you," I said happily. *What good timing! To be at my place for maybe an hour, and he calls.* I liked his clean-cut looks and had a good feeling about him. I agreed to a dinner date on Sunday night.

After returning to Langley Porter, I arranged my discharge, signing a paper stating I was leaving "against medical advice."

Len came for our date. I liked his soft, sensitive face, curly brown hair, and sense of humor. His blue eyes watched me intently during dinner and lit up when he smiled. He was thirty-five, Jewish, and liked his work as an attorney with a solo practice in Oakland.

I supposed he'd call again, but I had no expectations after dating for many years. I wondered what Len would have thought had he known I'd been home on a pass from a psychiatric hospital when he phoned.

17 – Staff Meeting

1975. San Francisco, California

Harry asked me to see him in his office on my first day after Langley Porter. Apprehensive, I took a deep breath and entered.

"Look, Marcia," he said. "Your behavior here frightened many people, and they have to know you're all right now and that they can trust you again. You'll need to hear their thoughts and feelings. So at tomorrow's staff meeting, after covering the agenda, during the open discussion time, I think this would be the best time if you're ready."

"I think I understand. They need to hear something from me." My throat felt tight. How would I face them and explain something I didn't know how to make sense of and wanted to forget?

"People care about you."

I felt my eyes misting and bit my lip not to cry. "Growing pains, right?" I said. Our eyes met, and we smiled.

At the staff meeting, about twenty-five of us sat in a circle of couches and chairs in the solarium. After completing the business agenda, Harry said, "This is a space to talk about people's feelings about Marcia and what happened recently."

Dick said, "First of all, welcome back, Marcia," and led the staff's applause. Everyone clapped.

What a guy, being so kind after I'd behaved so outrageously toward him. I felt warmed by all of them. "I'm glad to be back," I said.

"I'm glad you're back," said June.

"Marcia, welcome again," Dick said. "I actually enjoyed a lot about your behavior. I hope you'll let your spontaneous, fun nature shine more."

The truth was that I loved the freedom of saying whatever I felt like, being uninhibited instead of worrying about what people thought of me—like I was doing now, craving approval.

"It was also very frustrating for me," Dick continued. "I was trying to protect your rights but not getting an answer about what you wanted to do: go home, go to a hospital, or what. It was very hard."

"I was under a lot of pressure, between two sleepless nights and an all-day stressful personal situation—"

The agency's intake worker, Jeff, a former minister, said, "I want you to tell only as much as is comfortable for you."

"I want to hear the part related to work," added Dick. I liked that they were protecting me.

"Why didn't you ask for the support you needed?" Doreen asked.

I took a few deep breaths. "I realize I shouldn't have kept silent."

A recovering alcoholic paraprofessional, Pete, said, "I'm impressed by your insight and the similarity to my experience with drinking. I realized I needed to talk to people about things bothering me rather than drink. How similar things are."

I nodded in agreement. "I appreciate your sharing."

José, another recovering alcoholic staff member, said with his Mexican accent, "Remember that there's an important, creative, valuable part of your experience."

"I agree, and I value that part," I said, "and going crazy was fun. It's the ultimate in 'letting go.' It's like why I guess people take acid or some other drug to reach that kind of state, but I wish someone had taken me home and given me a pill to get to sleep. I was too hyped to ask for that, to know what I needed." I stopped to catch my breath and felt tears welling up. *Don't cry at a staff meeting.*

"I'm glad you're back," June repeated.

"I regret my lack of judgment, and especially that I'd gotten to the point where there was no better alternative than hospitalization."

Everyone seemed to take in my words; I felt they were all with me. Maybe not quite everyone, though. Some people who hadn't spoken looked empathic, but a few, like Stuart, the married rehabilitation counselor with whom my clinical supervisor, Don, had urged me to wrestle when I was depressed, seemed to gaze right through me. Their studied nonchalance seemed like they could have been watching a spectator sport with mild curiosity.

Steve had been uncharacteristically quiet, stealing an occasional glance at me. Mostly, he looked at the floor, his long, wavy hair flopping over his face. He shifted restlessly in his seat, sometimes tapping a foot.

"Marcia, I'm glad you're back," June said again. "I'd rather talk with you privately." Her sincerity and warm smile touched me.

"Me too," whispered Vicki, who sat beside me.

George, an internist who physically examined each inpatient, asked, "Can we move on to something else?"

I smiled to myself. He was a serious, overweight, married guy with two children, not into touchy-feely stuff. I liked his dry wit. Once, when someone asked him what type of patients he preferred to work with, without missing a beat, he'd said, "Attractive young women."

When the meeting was over, a new psych tech named Ben took one of my hands in both of his. "I don't know you very well, but I feel for you," he said, as tears filled my eyes.

Most of my coworkers responded with warmth and sensitivity. Then there was Steve, who not only spoke inappropriately about his sex life, he also had acted so sexually aggressive in our role-playing. Yet he couldn't face a discussion about my manic episode. Later, in our office, Steve busied himself at his desk, keeping his back to me.

So what? I can't worry about him. I need to concentrate on myself, notice what's happening in me before it gets out of hand, and regain my confidence.

Yet I wished I'd told him off, that I hadn't been too fragile to give him what he deserved.

18 – Mom's Zany Gesture

1975. San Francisco, California

While driving home, I thought the staff meeting went well, despite my fears. I felt loved and accepted. Harry was right. Putting the awkward topic on the table was a good idea, even if it left me vulnerable with my colleagues—like an "open book," a phrase my mother used when she wished she'd been more guarded instead of having answered a personal question.

I parked in front of my place. My landlady, Isma Michelli, single and in her sixties, lived upstairs. Her long-term boyfriend painted my apartment before I moved in. I loved it there, two blocks from the Marina Green and San Francisco Bay—like Rockaway, where our house was about the same distance from the ocean.

I gathered a few letters from the mailbox. Isma watched me from a window, and we waved to each other. She and I weren't close, but I sensed her concern. She knew I'd returned from my trip to New York about three weeks later than planned last year but had only asked, "Are you all right?"

Isma watched my comings and goings through her window. My friend Eileen once asked, "Don't you find it unnerving to have her watching so often?" Her question surprised me. I found Isma's presence comforting, and she didn't pry. I sensed she enjoyed my social life vicariously. Perhaps we were surrogate mother and daughter, but without the intensity of the real thing.

Inside, I set my mail on the kitchen table, put a tea kettle on the stove, and opened the curtains of the floor-to-ceiling window in my bedroom that looked out into the garden. Thanks to Isma's green thumb, roses in bloom were abundant. I'd show the garden to Len, I thought.

We'd made a date to see *Swan Lake* in San Francisco. I looked forward to seeing him again, with no expectations. I liked having someone to go out with; a relaxing performance of graceful dancers would make me forget everything else.

I sat at my kitchen table to sip tea and open mail. My mother's cheerful, loopy script stretched across an envelope, and I was glad to hear from her. After a second psychiatric hospitalization, and without her involvement this time, I felt less inclined to blame her for the first one.

I'd forgotten about the money she said to expect. So I was surprised to find a check for two thousand dollars along with her note. She wrote on a piece of yellow stationery with bright flowers:

"Here it is, sweetie. I believe in women's liberation, so you get the same as your sister. Remember, don't tell Gloria. I love you. Love, Mom."

I smiled at the idea of my mother as a women's libber. I couldn't picture her in a T-shirt with the slogan: "A woman needs a man like a fish needs a bicycle." Long after Dad married Ethel, she still said, "I gave him the best years of my life." She dated occasionally but continued to miss my father. Wouldn't a feminist have let go of wanting him long ago?

Most women my mother's age were portrayed as stuck, bored, miserable housewives in Betty Friedan's book, *The Feminine Mystique*, which helped launch the 1960s feminist movement. My mother wasn't that kind of woman. She said she returned to work when I was a toddler because she "was a scared bunny," what with my father always saying he wasn't happy and wanting to leave.

My mother's belief in women's liberation probably wasn't her reason for sending me the check. From the time when Gloria and I were little, my mother had this even-steven way of giving to us. "I do the same for both of you," she'd often said. "Whatever one gets, the other gets." She may have thought that giving each of us the same would prevent sibling rivalry; instead, it seemed to have bred a competition involving endless measuring between Gloria and me, to see if we were getting our fair share.

I remember crying at the dinner table one night when I was eight because I perceived Gloria's piece of cake to be bigger than mine. We compared everything. When Gloria was fifteen, she said, "Mom says you're *artistic*, and I'm *studious*, like I'm this dull, plodding type." Then she went upstairs in a huff over my getting the better deal.

"It's not fair. She got more," became our frequent complaint, which may have encouraged my mother to try harder to do the same for both of us. This equivalence pertained to allowance money, a shopping spree for clothing, or a new desk. So it must have been nagging at my mother for some time after Gloria's wedding that she gave her a big check and nothing to me.

I put the check in my desk drawer, in no hurry to cash it, enjoying my mother's gesture and the love behind it.

19 – Families

1975. San Francisco, California

Istood alone at the podium in a ballroom at the Sir Francis Drake Hotel, about to present my paper, "Homeostasis: A Key Concept in Working with Alcoholic Family Systems." Chandeliers hung from the ornate ceiling of the large room. As people drifted in, I wavered between thinking *I'm an expert* and *I'm an imposter.* I breathed in and out slowly, focusing on relaxing.

While plodding along to finish this paper and meet the National Conference on Alcoholism's submission date, I hadn't thought much about needing to present it if it got accepted.

When I told my mother I was nervous, she said, "Think of them in pajamas." I liked her idea. But as I scanned the accumulating audience, I felt more like I was in pajamas—*hospital pajamas.*

Besides feeling my usual public-speaking jitters, I still lived in dread that when stressed, something would cut loose inside me, and then I'd be, as Alan's words echoed, *carted off to a psychiatric ward.*

What if the mental health and alcoholism professionals rapidly filling the many rows of seats knew that the well-coifed woman in the tailored suit they came to hear had been locked up in psychiatric wards twice? Who knew when I might have another episode?

Doreen coordinated the submission of another paper, written by herself and five other colleagues, including Harry and Steve, which was rejected. I sensed befuddlement in them and myself. Why mine and not theirs? How come the nutty one gets in and not the sane ones? I imagined them scratching their heads. We were accustomed to dichotomies, labeling people as one thing or another, but what was I: crazy person, respected mental health expert, or what?

The room filled. I assumed my respected-expert identity, read my paper, responded to questions, and savored the applause.

In 1975 we didn't have personal computers or email attachments. Postcards began arriving in my mailbox; several requests daily for copies of my article, which I dutifully mailed out. I learned that my paper had become a reading assignment for graduate social work students at a university.

I sensed that many of my colleagues at work were watching and waiting, not ready to trust that I was really okay. I wondered if they feared subconsciously that if it—insanity—could happen to me, it might happen to them. I tried to detach myself from their judgments and do my job.

June and I continued to be Dick's co-therapists in the art therapy group, but he became more distant. I think he saw me as a time bomb that could go off any moment, jump into his lap, and try to tease him out of being gay.

Doreen, Steve, and I worked mainly with outpatients. Although we weren't alcoholics, we liked the population and its challenges. I provided individual, couples, and group therapy. Because many alcoholics started drinking again and stopped coming after a therapy session stirred up some anxiety, we had plenty of free time.

Most graduates of the agency's twenty-eight-day inpatient treatment program chose Alcoholics Anonymous over therapy. They thought a nonalcoholic therapist wouldn't understand them.

Doreen cut back to half-time after starting a private practice, which Carla helped her fill with referrals.

Steve put on extra weight when he acquired a new girlfriend, a clean-cut, sturdily built blond in her late twenties. "She likes me big," he said. After a while, he said she opted for a lesbian relationship.

Harry told Steve and me to reach out to community agencies to drum up business. Two social workers from an agency I contacted met with Steve and me.

We hit it off well. While making small talk, one woman remarked about all of us being Jewish. A few days later, Steve and the woman started dating. She seemed pleasant and normal. I supposed he hid his neuroticism from her.

Maybe she liked his charming, funny side. They got married. When she became pregnant, Steve got the jitters. "Should we get an abortion?" he asked me.

"No," I said. "Absolutely not." They had the baby. A year later, they divorced. I was sorry, especially for the baby, but not surprised.

I hated divorce. The fallout from my parents' divorce made it hard for me to accept it even as an abstract idea. I admired the couples who cared enough to come to therapy. Even though I tried to act neutral, the idea of an entirely objective therapist is a myth. *Stick it out,* I may have unconsciously telegraphed to my clients, with an unconscious flick of eyelashes, a faint smile, or a nod. Under my watch, none of my clients divorced.

The wife in one family I'd seen for therapy confessed to feelings of shame during a session with her husband and their thirteen-year-old son. "You probably don't see many as messed up as we are," she said. I'd often felt moved by their tenacity and willingness to be vulnerable with each other.

Departing from my usual reluctance to bring my personal life to a session, I said, "Your family is much healthier than the one I grew up in. And you care enough to keep working on making it better." My eyes misted. They appeared surprised, but all seemed to sit straighter in their chairs.

Afterward, as I wrote a few notes in their chart, I realized their son was the age I was when my parents divorced. I wished my parents had cared as much as these did. I sighed; virtually no one had heard of couples or family therapy before the 1970s.

I loved doing family therapy and evolved into our agency's expert in this field. I trained my interns to work with couples and families and helped two Protestant ministers, who spent some time at our agency, develop more skills in these areas.

I'd heard about multi-family therapy and considered starting a group of several families. "Don't do it," a colleague warned. "Save your energy." I started the group with an intern as my co-therapist. I liked leading it, and my energy was fine.

Families. Intact families. The more, the better.

20 – Telling Len

1975. Berkeley, California

Len and I had been dating for three months, a magic number in my mind. I'd been infatuated enough times to notice that the buzz would wear off within three months. If a friend told me she was in love with someone she had just met, I'd warn, "Wait three months, and see how you feel then."

Infatuation typically ends when an impossible flaw surfaces. If the relationship still thrives after three months, it might become *the real thing*.

I watched Len from a booth while he stood at the pizza restaurant counter to order. He wore Bermuda shorts that showed his muscular calves and well-shaped body. Len looked both strong and vulnerable. I felt love for him well up inside me like a current running through my chest, heart, and solar plexus. Three months had passed.

A few days after the pizzeria epiphany, I confided in Eileen while we sipped drinks in the corner of Len's dining room. Others at his party filled their plates at the buffet table while Len greeted new arrivals.

"I love his essence," I whispered.

"Wow!" she said. "That's how I felt about Alex. This could turn into something big."

Alex was Eileen's ex-boyfriend. They'd been living together for a year when I met her. Eileen's eyes glistened when she laughed, which was often. She had shoulder-length, thick, wavy blond hair and a healthy, curvy body. She was Jewish, and Alex was Protestant.

They seemed like a contented couple. I was eager to befriend Eileen because I wanted a role model of a good relationship, and theirs looked warm and caring. I visited them often in their apartment in the Twin Peaks district of San Francisco.

Back then, most of my friends and I were dreaming that whatever emotionally distant, commitment-phobic guy we were seeing would eventually come around. Eileen was a refreshing change.

"I don't know," I told her now. "I'm not sure how Len's going to feel about me if . . . I mean, there's something I think I should tell him, but I'm afraid to." *What am I doing telling* her? I asked myself. *She gossips. But I valued her opinion.*

Eileen was open about herself and expected others to reciprocate. I realized that she asked a personal question as casually as though asking about the weather and could spread the new information as though it were no more private than that.

"Something you don't know about. I need to know before I say anything that you'll keep it a secret." I was worried she would judge me once she knew, but I was more afraid she'd tell others. Enough people knew—my colleagues at work, my family, and some Rockaway neighbors. No need to announce it in a newspaper.

But what would Len think if I told him? Eileen was smart, practical, and experienced about relationships, although she was no longer with Alex. After telling her he wanted to experiment with other relationships, as recommended in the then-popular book, *Open Marriage*, Alex did. I was astounded when he phoned to ask me out. "No," I said. "Eileen is my friend." Eventually, he went off to live with another woman. Eileen ate enough to join Weight Watchers, then lost enough to become one of the organization's group leaders. "I'll never get over him," she said.

I wanted to tell Eileen about my hospitalizations now because I believed she could give a wise opinion about whether to tell Len. Psychiatric hospitalizations were still a hush-hush topic because of the stigma. Besides, I still hoped my episodes were more like accidents than recurring illnesses.

Not telling Len began to feel like lying. I needed to know whether he would feel different about me if he knew about my recent psychiatric events. He'd already said, "I love you," and soon after that, he asked me to move in with him.

I protested, "I don't want to feel like I'm living with the ghost of your ex-wife."

Len was vague about why she left him four years ago.

"You can redecorate so it will feel like your place; get new curtains," he said.

"You're used to being in charge here. You'll want to make all the decisions."

Len's house was a lovely example of Cape Cod architecture. He liked it and didn't want to move. And he wasn't ready to think about marrying again.

I felt vulnerable after Langley Porter and unprepared for any big change. So we were testing, talking, and creating a little distance between waves of intense feelings. But now I needed advice.

"I want to tell you," I said to Eileen. "Let's go upstairs where we can be alone."

We sat on single beds with matching quilted spreads in the guest bedroom. I liked the coziness of the upstairs and the intimate feeling of its sloped ceilings. I looked at my friend and took a deep breath.

"Something awful happened to me, and it's hard to explain . . ." I began. "Remember, this is not gossip. You won't tell anyone. Promise." She nodded, and I believed her. I had to.

I poured it all out about the two hospitalizations while she listened, her eyes growing wide in astonishment, then taking on a soft expression. Tears wet my face as I said shakily, "I want to tell Len, but I'm afraid it will change everything."

"I had no idea. You've been bearing this cross alone for a long time," she said. "You'll have to decide whether to tell him, but I doubt it will change his feelings."

"I don't know. Len thinks I'm so together. He says, 'You're so in touch with your feelings, so assertive.' He doesn't call me stubborn, and I know I can be; instead, he says, 'You have an *iron will*.' I've heard him sometimes refer to someone as 'crazy.' Does that mean he'll think I'm crazy—"

"No, no, no. Marcia! He will not think you are crazy. You are one of the sanest people I know. And he's right about your being assertive and in touch with your feelings." Her face took on a sly expression as she said, "But I disagree with the part about you having an iron will. Len was being nice. I think you are stubborn," she grinned.

I laughed and felt some tension drain.

"Marcia, you're great, and nothing can take that away from you. Really, I mean it, and you should believe me."

I looked at her gratefully, and we hugged.

"There you are, Marcia," said Len when we came downstairs. "I've been looking for you." He seemed happy to see me.

"Eileen and I had some catching up to do, you know, private stuff."

Len smiled, "Yeah, of course; I understand." I found how he nodded his head endearing.

When the last guest left, and Len and I were clearing dishes, I didn't want to wait another minute, fearing I'd chicken out. "Let's sit on the couch," I said. "We can do the rest later." We went into the living room, and he sat close to me. I moved away a bit, so we faced each other. He looked at me expectantly.

"I want to talk to you about this, but I'm afraid to. But I think it's important that you know . . . about something that happened to me."

Len looked at me with such tenderness that I sensed he expected something worse than my secret. I knew I'd better get this out fast, before I started bawling and couldn't speak. I wanted to look stable, not like someone who'd lose it under stress. I closed my eyes and breathed in and out before speaking.

"Last June, just before our first date, I had a difficult time. I hadn't slept for two or three nights, and my mind kept racing, and I became very agitated. I ended up in Langley Porter, on a psychiatric ward for four days." I rushed my story, wanting to get it over with and include all the facts. I paused. Len's face was soft as he took in my words, and his body was relaxed. "A year before, something similar happened to me in New York. But that time, I was in a place too awful to describe, a hospital, but you can't imagine. I was so overmedicated, I almost . . ."

Len looked at me steadily with kind eyes. He looked as though his heart was breaking for me. "I didn't want to tell you because I was afraid it would change things between us," I said, relieved to have it all out.

He spoke softly but firmly. "I love you very much." He moved closer, put his arms around me, and held me for a long time.

21 – Marriage Minded and Manic Again

1975. San Francisco, California

It was past dinnertime, but I was too excited to eat. Felt this way yesterday, too. Didn't sleep much last night or the night before. I was jumping inside my skin. Finally, after all the years of being single and looking for the right person. Big news! I had to tell someone. I sat at the edge of my waterbed, but my mind was flying.

I phoned Marian, my best friend. We were both still single after years of sharing dating stories, ever since we met as new social workers in San Francisco's Child Welfare Department.

"Marian, you're the first person I'm telling. Len and I are going to get married."

"Oh, Marcia, how wonderful! I'll give you a shower."

"Really?" How lucky I felt to have her in my life.

"Tell me more. When did you decide? How did it happen? Do you have a date set?"

"A long story, hard to explain, but I want you to know it's happening."

"I'm very curious, can hardly wait—"

"I'll tell you everything soon. Gotta call Len now."

I didn't call him right away, needing to calm down. My mind, on overdrive, registered that I felt a little scared, but not sure what of. All I knew was I needed to see Len right away.

After eleven, I phoned him. I was relieved to hear his voice.

"Len, I need to see you right now."

"What's going on?"

"I can't explain; I need to see you. It can't wait."

"I have a trial tomorrow, Marcia," he said in a patient, logical tone, which I ignored. I'd heard him sound this way, like he was humoring a petulant child.

"I need to see you."

"All right, Marcia. I'll be right over, but I can't stay long."

He's coming!

By the time Len arrived, I'd worked myself into a frenzy. He wore chinos and a golf shirt. I threw my arms around him and felt less frightened. I needed him close.

"Come over here," I said, pulling him a few steps toward my waterbed. "I'm so excited now that I know we're finally ready. Let's lie down here for a few minutes."

Len shook off my grasp. He stood in place, looking bewildered.

"Marcia, are you all right? You're talking a mile a minute. I feel like I'm caught in a whirlwind. What do you mean *ready*? Ready for what?"

"Come on; just hold me, and it'll be all right." Again, it seemed I was jumping out of my skin. I gently urged him onto the bed, pulling his arm until he joined me. I switched off the lamp. In the dark I felt a surge of relief.

"That's better. Oh, Len, I'm so glad we decided. We'll find a great place to live. You don't mind moving, do you? When we're married, it will be so much better in a new place for both of us—"

"Wait a min—"

"Can we have a dog? You know I always wanted a dog."

Len squirmed in the bed.

"Pleeease, just a little one, won't be too big, maybe medium—"

"Marcia, it's very late. I have a trial tomorrow. You're talking about important things; we can't decide everything right now. We haven't decided anything yet. You seem to be getting carried away—"

"I want to be carried away. I want you to carry me away. Marian said she'll give me a shower."

"Marcia, I have to go. We can talk about all this soon. It's very late, and I need to be in court by nine o'clock."

"It'll be okay. Just stay with me." I squeezed him tightly, never wanting to let him go. He felt so good, but he was trying to slip out of my arms. *Why does he want to go?*

"The judge can lock me up for contempt of court if I'm not there. I've got to get home, get some sleep—"

"Stay here. You can go straight from here in the morning."

"I need to sleep. It's a trial. I need to be rested, wear a suit—"

"But I need you here. I feel so—wired. It's hard to explain, but I'm frightened."

"Marcia, honey, I wish I could stay. Try to relax. I'll call you tomorrow." He rolled out of my arms and got up from the bed.

Shaking, I said, "I wish you could stay. There's so much to talk about. But remember about the dog, okay? The dog is very important. Please say yes about the dog."

"Marcia, I promise we'll talk about it all soon, but I *have* to go. You don't want me in jail, do you?"

He retreated to the entryway. I heard his faint "goodbye" as the door closed behind him. I stayed in bed, tossing and turning for some time.

My mind continued racing. *What will it be like being married to Len? Will we have a dog? Be okay together? What if we're not? Of course, we'll be. He loves me. I love him. But what if—I know who I have to talk to—the psychology graduate students I'd supervised, Elizabeth and Julie. They just finished their internships.*

I looked at their thank-you gift on my dresser: a large, hand-thrown, sparkling blue-and-white ceramic bowl they'd surprised me with on their last day at work. They felt like dear friends. Both had live-in boyfriends, so they knew about relationships. They could make sense of what was happening, reassure me, and calm me down.

I turned on the lamp and dialed Elizabeth's number, unaware it was after two a.m. *If she can't come now, I'll call Julie.*

Elizabeth answered, sounding groggy. I rambled about getting married, not sleeping or eating much in the last few days, and being afraid to be alone. She said she would come over.

She arrived with Julie; they had become close friends. They had already scheduled an emergency appointment with a psychiatrist in Pacific Heights. He was a clean-cut, young man who sat behind his desk, wearing a button-down shirt and a tie. Still agitated, I felt safe with the three of them, like I was in good hands. The doctor advised me to sign a form to admit me to McAuley Neuropsychiatric Institute as a voluntary patient. He made the arrangements.

I signed the form. My former students drove me there.

22 – With Help from Friends

1975. San Francisco, California

Dr. Hollander, my psychiatrist at McAuley Neuropsychiatric Institute, looked in his forties. Handsome in a Paul Newman kind of way, he seemed caring. I trusted him. But when he suggested lithium, I hesitated. Yet this was my third hospitalization in a year and a half. I could no longer deny my problem.

I caught up on sleep after a couple of days at McAuley. The effects of the heavy tranquilizer were wearing off. Although I signed in as a voluntary patient, I didn't ask to leave. I agreed with Dr. Hollander that something needed to change if I didn't want to keep getting hospitalized.

On my third morning there, Dr. Hollander pulled up a chair next to mine in the ward's lounge. "Look, it's your decision," he said, "but I urge you to consider lithium. It evens out the highs and lows and has helped many people." This idea no longer sounded as absurd as when the Langley Porter psychologist introduced it.

Still, I was uncomfortable about starting lithium. Would taking it mean I was truly crazy?

"Just try to keep an open mind," Dr. Hollander added. I liked his concerned, respectful manner.

"I'll try to," I smiled, wanting to be a good patient for him.

After he left, an attendant said, "I have a message from your friends." She gave me a piece of paper taken from a small, loose-leaf notebook. Eileen's handwriting was on one side:

Dear Marcia,

Marian and I have talked to Dr. Hollander. We feel much better about everything. We hope you'll soon be feeling better, and we'll come and visit you as soon as we're allowed to. Dr. Hollander seems very sympathetic.

I love you, Marcia, and I still believe in you and will be your friend when you get out. Len also stands behind you and wants to see you as soon as he's permitted to. Marian wants to see you too.

Love,

Eileen

The note on the other side was from Eileen's sister, Carol:

Dear Marcia,

I love you & I hope we can see you soon. If you act calm, they'll let us see you.

Love,

Carol

That evening, they returned, and the three of us conversed in a cozy room. I sat on a couch and tried on the fuzzy, bright-pink slippers Carol brought me. They looked huge because they were so fluffy. I smiled each time I looked at my feet.

"We talked to your doctor," said Eileen. "We think you should try the lithium; we really want you to."

Carol, who was visiting Eileen from her community of transcendental meditators in Iowa, looked soulfully into my eyes and nodded. "Please take it. We think he knows what he's doing." She beamed with tenderness, and her eyes looked like they were welling up with tears, as though it would break her heart if I didn't take the medicine.

"I don't know. I don't want to have to go through this again. I'm thinking about it." I felt ashamed in my hospital gown. My visiting friends did not have psychotic episodes that caused them to get hauled off routinely to places like this.

But more than that, I felt their love. The pink slippers said it all.

Len visited a little later, after dinner. He sat on the mattress of an unmade bed next to mine. He too had talked with Dr. Hollander. Looking steadily into my eyes, he said, "Try the lithium. Please." My jaw tightened at the mention of lithium. "I love you, and I want you to be okay."

I met his eyes. I saw the adoration in them and relaxed my jaw. "Okay," I nodded. "Okay. I'll try it."

When Len visited two days later, I'd taken three pills daily. Dr. Hollander said I could leave when my blood reached a stable lithium level. A week after being admitted, Dr. Hollander said I was ready to be discharged and return to work as long as I continued taking the pills.

When I phoned Harry to tell him I'd be at work the next day, he said I should take a week off to make sure I was okay.

"Dr. Hollander says I'm ready, that I'm fine now, and as long as I take the lithium, there should be no problem."

"I'd like to have something in writing from him to make sure." Harry sounded skeptical, which made no sense to me. He'd let me come back with no expressed reservations the last two times. Now that I was finally on medication, he wanted to be cautious?

"Okay. I'll ask him to write a note for you."

Dr. Hollander wrote the letter for Harry, stating my lithium level was stable, he trusted me to continue taking it, and he saw no reason why I couldn't return to work immediately.

I put the note on Harry's desk before he arrived. Half an hour later, he called me into his office. He looked uncomfortable, almost shaken.

"You're not ready to be here. You've had three psychiatric hospitalizations within a year. You need to take a break, at least a week off."

"Not a year. A year and a half," I corrected him. He shrugged. "Did you read Dr. Hollander's letter?"

"Yes, I read it." He frowned. "That letter doesn't mean anything. It's political."

Did he think that Dr. Hollander was just being nice? I stared at Harry, speechless.

"Look, I'm just not comfortable with you here now. You can use a week's sick leave. I'll approve it."

I looked at him, unbelieving, and shook my head. "I'm not sick. I don't want to take sick leave, and I don't need to rest. I've had lots of time to rest."

"Then I have to insist." Harry's jaw was set. "I will not change my mind. Please do not argue with me about it. I find you intimidating."

Intimidating! I was furious with him for trying to delay my return to work, and who was he to make me use up sick days after he was so laissez-faire about anything I did regarding work, including letting me use sick days for skiing? And now he was saying he felt *intimidated* by me.

Soon after I'd started the job four years earlier, Harry humiliated me by saying behind his closed office door: "People here perceive you as timid and naive." *Timid and naive.* Was I? It *had* been a culture shock to experience that let-it-all-hang-out environment when I first came to work there. I'd promptly heard Steve reveal his sexual performance problem, been hugged in a long, lingering way by a male paraprofessional who seemed to be taking advantage of the touchy-feely climate at the agency, and experienced Doreen's lukewarm reception.

Timid and naive. I knew there was more to me than that, but after Harry said my coworkers viewed me that way, I felt more uncomfortable around him and my new colleagues for some time.

And now, *intimidating.* This was a new label for me.

23 – Mother's Expectations

My mother used to say I had *a mean streak*, a term she had used to describe me when we still lived in Brooklyn. I was five years old and near the kitchen sink. Upset with my mother over some trifle, I screamed, "I hate you!"

"You have a mean streak," she shot back. She mentioned my mean streak again a couple of times while I was very young, saying to a friend after I must have shown hostility, "Marcia has a mean streak."

I learned to be *good*; I didn't rebel. I knew not to complain when I felt smothered by my mother's goodnight kisses after my father left us. I cringed inside and felt used. Who were the kisses meant for? My father? Her mother, whom she still visited but I'd never met? Or possibly Morris, the father she'd never known? My chest would tighten. I felt not love but her neediness.

But Mom was also my biggest cheerleader. When a friend phoned, she sometimes said, "Marcia, it's your public calling," like I was famous. She also would announce, "Marcia was born in *California*," as though I had accomplished something marvelous. And I felt proud of that.

*From left: Dad, Gloria, me, and Mom
in California, soon after I was born.*

Both of my parents were New Yorkers. Mom was pregnant with me when she and Gloria moved to Oakland to join Dad, an army air force officer stationed there during World War II. While that war was winding down, the one between my parents began. My mother said my father started straying during this pregnancy.

After finishing graduate school, I thought about moving to California. Most single young women from Rockaway who wanted a social life moved to Manhattan. Gloria had found a comfortable, rent-controlled walk-up in a prime neighborhood, half a block from the glitzy Plaza Hotel. But I didn't care for Manhattan's soot-filled air and noisy traffic punctuated by emergency vehicles' sirens all night.

I was still deciding where to settle when Gloria introduced me to Mindy. "Mindy and I were assigned as roommates at a

Jewish singles weekend at Grossinger's about three years ago. We hit it off," Gloria said, as we walked to Schrafft's for lunch. "Not only did I meet Mindy but she also met her husband there."

"Oh, well, at least I met you," she smiled at Mindy.

"Better than nothing," Mindy laughed, revealing pearly-white teeth.

I quickly felt like Mindy was my friend too. She was willowy and pretty, with hair that fell to her shoulders in soft, brown waves that shimmered in the sunlight. A few men's heads turned to stare at her as we moved along the crowded sidewalks. She was bubbly and talked as though she'd known me for years.

Mindy's face glowed while we continued along the busy streets as she talked about her husband. Over the roar of buses, honking horns, and doormen's taxi whistles, she said, "Our sex life wasn't so great in the beginning, but we work on it, and it's improving." I listened and forgot about the crowds and noise. I'd never heard anyone refer to marriage as something you work on.

I thought marriage was either a fairy-tale, happily-ever-after state or its opposite, like my parents' marriage and the unhappy marriages of my mother's friends and acquaintances. Mindy implied that marriage could be something else—not perfect, yet sweet and happy overall.

The three of us, and the servers, were the youngest in Schrafft's, by a couple of decades. As we ate, I gathered that these well-heeled customers enjoyed its salads, sandwiches, and sundaes. Also, its rich, dark, wood-paneled walls, white table cloths, and timeless, quiet atmosphere.

Seeing the older women made me wonder how my mother, now fifty-five, would feel about my moving far away. Maybe their presence also made Mindy think of her mother. As our lunches arrived, she said, "I couldn't have married if I hadn't stopped letting my mother control me."

"What do you mean?" I asked.

"She subtly suggested I wasn't good enough to get a husband. One day, when I was alone, I said to myself, *I am not going to let you destroy me.*" Mindy stabbed a cherry tomato in her salad with a fork.

I was impressed by Mindy's strength of will.

My mother was different, though—my biggest supporter. She bragged about and exaggerated my accomplishments. She'd tell her friends, "Marcia is the editor of her high school newspaper." She persisted, no matter how many times I corrected her, saying, "I'm not the editor; I'm the *feature editor*." She made me feel like I could do almost anything.

I grew up without rules, curfew, or protests about my choice to attend Harpur College, now Binghamton University, in Binghamton, New York. Gloria and most of our friends lived at home and went to Brooklyn College.

Yet, in a way, when it came to dating, my mother gave me a similar message to Mindy's. She expected me either to stay single or to fail at marriage. Her frequent question, "Is he still nice?"—asked about anyone I was dating, said it all: *Has he shown his ugly side yet?*

Given the poor track records of her father and her husband, where would she have developed a trust in men? Ten years after the divorce, my mother's pain still filled the air like a permanent mist. When Dad came to Rockaway to take Gloria and me to dinner, she continued to look like she'd been kicked. I flinched when she probed me for facts about Ethel and their daughter.

It was true when I replied, "I don't know," to my mother's questions. My father compartmentalized his life, speaking little of his new family with Gloria and me. I was barely conscious of having a half-sister, fourteen years younger. Had I had answers for my mother, they would have only added salt to her wounds. Yet I sensed I was disappointing her by not being her spy.

Because I had lost touch with my emotions long ago, except for feelings of guilt, I lacked the vocabulary to tell her that such questions pained me. I wished she would stop asking, but I never said so. How could I have? That would have been *mean*.

I was similarly conflicted whenever I contemplated leaving New York. How could I be so selfish to leave my mother after all she'd been through? I feared she would be devastated to have me so far away. So, I had gradually and casually told her I might move to California. I wrote from graduate school at the University of Michigan that a former college roommate raved about San Francisco after spending last summer there, which was true. I occasionally dropped more hints to help her get used to the idea of my moving.

All this history and future yearnings swirled in my head as I admiringly watched Mindy. As the waitress at Schrafft's brought our sundaes in old-fashioned, ice-cream glasses, I said I was nervous about moving but didn't mention my mother. "I've heard great things about San Francisco—the weather, the social life, the clean air—but I don't know anyone there, don't have a job—"

"San Francisco is wonderful," gushed Mindy. "If you go, I can tell you where to stay—the Ansonia. It's a residence club. I was there for several days when I was traveling around California. Young professionals from all over stay there when they first move to San Francisco."

"I liked San Francisco too," Gloria added. She spooned up some whipped cream, nuts, hot fudge sauce, and ice cream and tasted it, satisfied. "It has a lot of areas like parts of New York, but everything's smaller—smaller theater district, smaller Chinatown, smaller downtown." Gloria had taken a Greyhound bus across the country with a friend after graduating from Brooklyn College. She said the only place that had something special New York didn't have was Cheyenne, Wyoming, because of the cowboys and Old West atmosphere.

"I stayed there as a tourist about four years ago," Mindy said. "I still remember it's at 711 Post Street, a quiet location close to downtown. You can stay there until you find an apartment."

I jotted the address on a napkin, tucked it in my purse, and finished my sundae, saving the cherry for last.

My mother needs me, I thought, on the subway to Rockaway. At college, I'd never felt far from my mother. Every day, a usually cheerful letter arrived from her, sometimes two.

That night, I broached the subject of California, hemming and hawing a bit as we talked at the kitchen table. "I'm not sure I'll do it; I'm just thinking about it. You know how you always talked about me being born there and all? For a long time, I thought maybe I'd like to try living there, and now that I'm ready to take a job—"

"California sounds exciting," she said, pausing for another bite of apple pie. "You can see if you like it without deciding to move," she said. "Just take a suitcase and think of it as a vacation. You can always come home. I'll send the rest of your things if you like it there and want to stay."

I started packing the next day.

The Ansonia Residence Club lived up to Mindy's praise. I met other recent arrivals over tasty meals served in its dining room. Some of us played ping-pong near the dining area. A guy I sometimes played with made copies of my résumé at the print shop where he worked.

The bathroom was down the hall from my room, which had a sink, and the rent included maid service.

After four weeks and several job offers I hadn't accepted, I was almost out of money. Then the boxes arrived, filled with what my mother was supposed to send *after* I said I was staying.

But she'd sent everything, even my skis. *Oh, Mom, how could you? I thought I was supposed to be in charge of this California experiment. You weren't the one who had a problem with me leaving; I was the one who wasn't quite ready.*

She'd sent a letter, too, advising me to "find happiness every day. Store up the good times to shore you up during the rough ones."

I began my social work career at San Francisco's Child Welfare Department. The work was meaningful, and the supervision was terrific. I formed lasting friendships there, including with my best friend, Marian; my ski buddy, Mimi; and Betty, who lived near me. My new life in San Francisco was going well.

I asked my mother many years later, "Why did you send my things to San Francisco before I gave the word?"

She said, "It was time to cut the umbilical cord."

24 – My Mother's First Visit

1969. San Francisco, California

My mother carried two heavy suitcases from baggage claim. She dropped them so we could hug. *Had she gotten shorter?* When I bent to kiss her, I smelled her perfume.

Before her plane landed, she must have spritzed perfume behind her ears, like she taught me to do as a teenager. I pictured her taking a compact from her purse and dabbing on rouge and peachy-red lipstick. She wanted to look nice for me.

"Hi, Mom, it's so good to see you," I smiled, eager to show her my life in California.

"You look wonderful, Marcia."

"Let me help you," I offered but strained when trying to lift a suitcase. Instead, I draped her purse over my shoulder. It weighed me down.

"Ugh. How do you do it, Mom?"

"I'm used to it. They balance each other." She grabbed one in each hand, and we walked toward an escalator. "Go ahead, sweetie," she said, for me to go before her.

Sweetie. My chest tightened. I didn't want her to call me that. I wanted to be me, to feel like an adult with her. I didn't want to be what she wanted: an eternally perfect, sticky-sweet girl.

I thought things should be different between my mother and me. She'd be in my apartment for a week, and I'd take us places in *my* car. The last time she was my passenger was when I was twenty and learning to drive. Usually, my father gave me lessons, which went smoothly. It was different with my mother. After I had accelerated Mom's Rambler up to ten miles per hour, she screamed, "Slow down! That's dangerous."

As my mother lugged her baggage onto the escalator, I marveled at her strength. Despite her "delicate digestive system," resulting from an ulcer that caused the removal of two-thirds of her stomach, she might have been stronger than most men her age and some younger ones.

My mother's large purse probably held snacks: cottage cheese, carrots, celery sticks, and apples. She said she took food with her always because her condition required her not to be hungry for long.

Photos from her younger days showed her looking trim, at least thirty pounds lighter. Her body had widened, but it still served her well. She danced effortlessly and demonstrated splits and somersaults to the girls in her junior high school gym classes.

"Can I help you?" asked a young man behind my mother on the escalator.

Turning her head, she quipped, "No thanks; women's lib."

This cracked me up. My mother, the women's libber.

As we rode the hills of Franklin Street toward my place in my peppy, beige 1966 122s Volvo, she said, "You drive like a cowboy." I smiled, feeling gutsy and not sweet. She was a slow, erratic driver suspected of causing several accidents for which she blamed drivers who rear-ended her car for driving too close.

I still had not bought much furniture at this point. My end tables were orange crates with wooden slats, and my bookcase was made of bricks and boards. My trundle bed doubled as a couch. I wheeled the extra bed to the opposite wall for my mother's visit.

"Your place is lovely," my mother said, admiring the garden view. She didn't mention the crates or the lack of a television, but the next day, she bought me a Zenith twelve-inch, black-and-white TV that fit neatly on my bookcase's top shelf. I loved that she got me the television, which I hadn't gotten around to or missed.

"When you write my memoirs, you can include how much I like your new home," my mother said.

Aggh! I felt my chest tighten. Since I was seventeen and feature editor of Far Rockaway High School's newspaper, my mother had occasionally said I'd write her memoirs. Why on earth would I want to do that? Did she think I owed her that because she grew up in an orphanage, and I didn't?

I was not going to write my mother's memoirs. If only I had been able to tell her she should write them herself, but I stayed silent. After all she'd been through, how could I tell her the truth?

Mom and I became too busy for me to dwell on that discomfort. We enjoyed our San Francisco sightseeing trips to Coit Tower in Telegraph Hill, North Beach, Chinatown, Union Square, and Twin Peaks. We shopped for clothes and had lunch at a Chinese restaurant in Ghirardelli Square, where my mother bought us matching, bright-yellow acrylic turtlenecks knit in a striped pattern. We had a lovely time together.

When I returned from my job as a child welfare worker the next day, my mother had covered the orange crates with gift-wrap paper she bought a few blocks away on Chestnut Street. "Thanks, Mom. They look elegant now," I said, tongue in cheek, not minding at all.

I wanted to impress my mother, but she wanted to tell me to drive slower, eat more protein, and get rid of a guy I liked. A lawyer I invited for dinner joked around with her. She told me he was "nervy," spoiling my good feelings for him. I couldn't see him differently from how she did.

I hated myself for resenting her, when she had come across the country to see me; she was trying to help and loved me so much. And she was proud of me. "Social workers are next to G-d," she'd said, having heard this somewhere.

On her last day at my place, when I came home from work, I saw the faucets in the bathroom sink were removed, and various hardware pieces sat in the basin. "Mom," I said, feigning patience, "What happened?"

"Don't worry," she said, stretched out on her bed, resting. "I talked to your landlady, and she's sending a plumber. I told her I'd pay—"

"But how—"

"The faucet was leaking. I thought I could fix it."

How could she be so destructive? She knew nothing about plumbing. But she was trying to help. Why must she take over? Can't she at least ask me first? In my apartment, she involved my landlady, aggh!

Finally, I said, "Why couldn't you leave it alone? What do you know about plumbing?" And then her face took on that crushed-little-girl look. I could never bear to see that hurt expression; she looked like a broken doll when she thought I was rejecting her.

I was furious and fought back the tears.

My mother, sitting up now, must have read my feelings.

Overcome by guilt, I said, "That's okay, Mom. I know you were trying to help."

I went into the bathroom, closed the door, and cried quietly into the useless sink.

25 – Betrayals

1975. San Francisco, California

Back at work, after Harry insisted on my taking a week of sick leave following my discharge from McAuley, I realized it was open season on me again. Steve was in the office when I came in to replace a client's chart. He grinned wickedly. "I know what you're taking," he called. Then Steve danced a little jig and sang: "It starts with an 'L' then an 'I,' then a 'T,' then an 'H' and an 'I' and 'U' and 'M.' Put it all together! What do ya get? Lithium!" he shouted triumphantly while a secretary ignored him from her desk.

My face burned. Steve's laughter trailed behind me as I left.

A day or so later, Stuart, the handsome, married rehab counselor with whom the psychiatrist, Don, suggested I wrestle, approached me in the hall. He said, "It's funny; I never used to feel this way about you, but lately, I find you sexually attractive."

Quaking inside, I turned my blandest clinical face toward him and said nothing. I moved him out of my mental file of safe people, put him into the one for predators, and gave him a wide berth.

Jeff, the former minister, and his wife had recently adopted a baby. I supervised him clinically regarding his performance as an intake worker. We'd enjoyed a respectful, professional relationship until he asked me, "What if a supervisee wants to sleep with his supervisor?"

Et tu, Brute? "How would your wife feel about that?" I countered weakly, caught off guard again.

"She got what she wanted," he said with an edge. *Of course, the baby*, I thought ironically, *an even exchange.*

Feeling confused and overwhelmed by these colleagues' harassment, I learned to distance myself from the perpetrators. Vicki and June, my faithful friends with whom I ate lunch frequently, were the exceptions. I felt grateful to them for holding fast to our friendship.

June and I started a psychodrama group for inpatients. We had a blast as co-therapists, playing charades with the patients, who laughed while learning to cut loose and have fun without alcohol.

Every evening, Eileen phoned me to check in. She understood the situation at work and helped me keep chugging along. "Free-floating hostility," she called it. "It lands wherever it senses weakness."

She also knew I was feeling groggy much of the time and thought it was from the lithium. "Talk to your doctor," she said. "Maybe he'll tell you to take less medicine."

I did, and Dr. Folger, whom I was seeing now for therapy, gradually lowered my dose from three pills a day to one.[4]

Alert again, I thought things weren't going well between Len and me. "I don't think he wants anything serious," I told Eileen on the phone, sitting on my couch, surrounded by pillows and my Red Riding Hood doll.

"Len really cares for you. He was there for you when you were in the hospital, visiting and all."

----

4   Readers taking psychotropic medication are strongly urged to make changes *only under the supervision of a knowledgeable professional* who prescribes and carefully monitors your medication. There have been disastrous results, including fatalities, for too many mentally ill people who decided to discontinue a potentially life-saving medication without medical supervision.

"Well . . . yes, but do you know what he said when I asked why he came to see me at McAuley only twice? He said, 'I didn't know how long you would be there.' It was like he thought I might be there for a long time, and he didn't want to start a pattern of daily visits that he'd feel obligated to continue."

"So?"

"Well, it feels cold. If Len were serious about me, I think he'd have come daily, like a husband would, and not worry about overextending himself."

"Um. I can see how you'd feel that way, but he *did* come and talk to Dr. Hollander. I know he was concerned. You might be expecting too much; think about that."

"You know what else? What do you think he said when I brought up the subject of where our relationship is going?"

"That he's not ready?"

"He said—" I began to choke up. "He said, 'Let's see how the lithium works.' Like I was the subject of some experiment instead of someone he wanted to marry."

"You can understand how he'd want to be cautious." She was logical and practical, but no, I didn't understand.

Dr. Folger monitored my lithium and ordered routine tests to ensure that the right amount of medicine was in my blood. He was also my therapist and not the kind who mainly listened. He shared his opinions freely.

About my mother, he said, "Don't let her pull that orphanage crap on you."

And about Len, "He sounds like a *gaslighter*."

"What's a gaslighter?" I asked.

"The expression comes from the name of a movie where a man tortures a woman emotionally, making her doubt her perceptions until she thinks she's crazy."

But I didn't view Len that way. Mostly, he was kind and acted like he loved me. At least he said so and kept seeing me, even if he was vague about the future.

Yet, he could be a bit cruel. When we were driving back from Santa Cruz, I was wearing a light shift and said I was cold and wanted him to stop so I could get my jacket from the trunk. He said it wasn't cold, and he was unwilling to pull out of heavy traffic when it was already getting late. I sulked and became aloof until he wormed his way back into my good graces with flowers and sweet talk.

The big showdown came after I returned from an out-of-town, weekend professional conference. I missed Len and phoned him late that Saturday night, but he didn't answer.

The following Tuesday, we walked from my place to Marina Joe's on Chestnut Street. After we ordered dinners, I pumped him for information.

"I phoned you after ten Saturday night, when the last meeting ended, but there was no answer."

"Oh, I must have been out for a while," he said, sounding deliberately vague. I glanced around at the couples seated at tables and booths and noticed wedding rings on most of the women, who seemed about my age. I was thirty-one. They looked content, husbands and wives enjoying a meal out.

I turned back toward Len. He squirmed in his seat, then stared at the grill where the chef tossed together the ingredients for Joe's Special, a mixture of ground beef, spinach, scrambled eggs, onions, and mushrooms. When he returned his gaze to me, I asked the question whose buzzing in my ear was getting louder.

"Were you out with a woman?"

He swallowed. "Well, yes, actually I was," he said. His tone was defensive, perhaps anticipating where my questioning would end.

"As soon as I'm gone, you go out with someone else?"

"Marcia, it was Saturday night. I wanted to go out, and you were gone. What's the big deal?"

"So, where did you go?"

"We went to dinner," Len said, in a long-suffering tone, as though responding to a child's question that didn't deserve an answer.

"Did you sleep with her?"

He looked down. "Marcia!"

"Well, did you?"

He was silent. Suddenly, the grill on which the food was being cooked fascinated him.

"You did!" I could hardly breathe. "How could you?"

"It didn't mean anything. It was just a date—"

"Just a date! The one time I'm away on a Saturday night, you have to go and have sex with someone." I was so furious. "I've got to get out of here," I said, more loudly than intended.

Len glanced around nervously, aware of heads turning. He whispered, "You're making a big thing over noth—"

I grabbed my purse and raced out as the waiter brought our plates. Len ran after me and caught up. "You're being ridiculous."

"Oh, sure. It's all me, and you're just fine. The minute I go away, you—"

"Just come back inside. Let's eat, and we can talk—"

"I need to be alone. I'm going home. You go back inside if you want, but don't follow me."

"But Marcia . . ." I could hear the hurt in his voice and liked knowing he cared enough for me to feel pain. But I had to get away before he lulled me into thinking that what he had done was okay. "Please . . ."

"I mean it. Let me go." He shrugged as though to say, "Have it your way." I walked down Fillmore Street toward my apartment.

During the following weeks, Len and I argued about what I felt was a betrayal and he viewed as trivial. We got nowhere because we were operating under different moral codes. Neither of us was able to make sense of the other's.

I thought we had an agreement, even if we'd never voiced it. If he seriously cared for me, I couldn't imagine how he could have felt free to sleep with someone else. He said it had nothing to do with how he felt about me.

I no longer trusted him. I hurt so much that, finally, I said I wanted to take a break from seeing him. He accused me of punishing him. He phoned periodically to keep in touch but never apologized; instead, he implied I was unreasonable. I told him not to call. Yet I missed him for a long time.

The lithium was working. Over a year since starting on it, I was okay at work, if not winning any popularity contests. Then came Harry's big announcement at a staff meeting: Because of a massive, soon-to-be-implemented cutback in state funding, our treatment center would soon lose two-thirds of its budget, most of which went for salaries.

The legislators had decided to save money by funding agencies staffed mainly by recovering alcoholics who lacked professional credentials. They cut funding for our treatment center, where many well-paid staff members had advanced degrees and were not recovering alcoholics. Two social work jobs would be eliminated in two months.

Doreen was in private practice full-time by then. Her replacement, Evelyn, was a gray-haired, divorced social worker in her early sixties. Her job and mine were on the chopping block, leaving Steve as the agency's only social worker.

A week after Harry's announcement, Bruce Merton, a former Child Welfare Department colleague, phoned to ask me to work in San Francisco General Hospital's psychiatry department, where he was the chief social worker.

I told Bruce, "I was there when I was looking for my first job in San Francisco." I rolled my eyes at the thought, picturing the decrepit, faded-brick institutional building. I remembered, upon entering the dimly lit psychiatric ward that day long ago, seeing a slovenly-looking older female patient in the hallway who lay ignored on a wooden bench in an apparent stupor. Disheveled hair spilled across her face, and her hospital gown was scrunched around her hips, revealing flabby thighs and sagging underpants.

Fighting back tears, I'd endured the interview with a pleasant, well-dressed woman seated across the desk from me and avoided asking her the troubling question: *How do you stand working here?*

Well into my career eight years later, why would I want to set foot inside that dreadful place again?

As though reading my mind, Bruce said, "It's much nicer here now. We've just moved into a new building."

I scheduled a time to meet with him.

26 – Keeping Secrets from Mom

1976. San Francisco, California

When my mother phoned, I was glad to hear her voice. "What's cooking?" she asked.

"Nothing much." If I mentioned Len, she'd warn me again about lawyers (they argue too much). If she knew I was in a relationship, she'd ask, once again, "Is he still nice?"

I had stopped telling my mother about men in my life since our estrangement. Maybe she thought I'd given up on them. She had suggested a while ago that I get a dog and hinted she'd be okay if I became a lesbian. "Anything to cuddle with," she said.

"They say no news is good news, and you sound good," my mother said. "Oh, do you know where I was last weekend? You'll never guess. I stayed at the Waldorf Astoria. For a Dance Educators of America convention. It was wonderful. I went to workshops and learned some new dances."

"Sounds like fun."

Better not to mention Langley Porter, either. Why upset her? I should share no more of my private life with her than I would with a near stranger. I want to see her objectively and keep my views instead of letting hers influence mine.

"I even got to lead a workshop. Someone canceled at the last minute. When they asked for a volunteer, I taught them the Alley Cat. They loved it as much as my junior high girls. You should have seen them doing the steps!"

"Great, Mom!"

I felt like her cheerleader. She wanted my approval so often, wanted everyone's. So easy to lose myself in her neediness. No room for me. My mind drifted to Len because I was still heartsick.

"Stomping their feet, clapping their hands in time to the music. Good thing I brought the tape along. I wore my black circle skirt with sparkly sequins and a red velvet cape. They all clapped for me when it was over. I spun and bowed; someone called out, "Bravo!"

"Wonderful." I pictured her curtsying, one foot bent behind the other, looking like a rouge-cheeked doll, smiling sweetly, savoring the applause.

Thoughts of Len returned. I couldn't accept his betrayal. I missed him and had to numb myself to prevent rekindling our relationship.

"They called me the unsinkable Mollie Brown. One of the men I've known for a long time, a ballroom dance teacher, said, 'Everyone gets older but Mollie.'"

Again, I was swept into her world. "Ha, ha. It's true, Mom." At sixty-three, she had more stamina than I did.

"And when I went to the gynecologist yesterday for a check-up, he said that my sexual organs are like those of a woman twenty years younger."

Please no! I don't want to hear about your sexuality.

She returned to the dance educators weekend. Half-listening, I rubbed a finger over the bumps and depressions of my gold ring, as though trying to erase something. Helped by a dental student who had access to the gold, I designed it when I was twenty-seven. It looked like a wedding band, so I wore it on my right hand.

If Len truly wanted to marry me, would I have been willing? We fought about petty issues, like what restaurant to go to for dinner. I imagined we'd battle about where to live. Would Len cheat after marriage and blame me for holding it against him?

My mother kept talking. I felt the bumps on my ring again and twirled it around my finger.

"Marcia, are you there? It's quiet on your end."

I snapped to attentiveness. "I'm listening, Mom." I hadn't tuned in to the details but grasped the gist of her monologue: The food at the Waldorf was gourmet, with rib-eye steaks served at the banquet. She and the other dance educators laughed, kicked up their heels, and had a grand time. And they loved her Alley Cat.

"You were the life of the party, Mom."

27 – Mom's Liberation

1957. Rockaway, New York

"I loved sports," my mother said, when she told me more about her life at the orphanage. "I was a champion on the uneven parallel bars. Oh, and of course, I loved dancing. Did I ever tell you how I invented the Rope Dance?"

"How?"

"It's funny, because that dance made it possible for me to go to college in a round-about way."

"Mm," I murmured, encouraging her to explain.

"It's a long story. The Academy's trustees wanted us to be self-sufficient and learn a trade, and the administrators made the girls take classes to prepare us for garment trades, the kitchen, or the business office."

The Academy. The name suited the institution because, in some ways, the Hebrew Orphans Asylum, or H.O.A., was like a well-endowed private school with modern facilities.

"My friend, Esther, your 'Aunt Esther,' was an exception. And by the skin of my teeth, I got to be an exception too.

"Esther was lucky because her mother convinced the authorities to let her take academic classes with the smart boys. She was only six when her father died from tuberculosis. Her mother was too poor to take care of her, so she placed her in the orphanage. Esther always had her nose in a book.

"Esther's mother pleaded with the administrators to let her daughter take academic classes. She wanted Esther to go to college."

Wistfully, my mother added, "I wish I'd had a mother to do that for me."

My mother attended a public high school on the Academy's grounds because it had so many students. "They put me in sewing, homemaking, and stenography classes. I hated them all."

Then she described her daring escape from domestic prison, one day in sewing class.

1927. The Academy

It is 1927. Mollie is fourteen. After placing her notebook on her work table, she looks around the room. Thick rolls of fabric in various colors lean against one wall; a row of sewing machines faces the opposite one. *What am I doing here?* she wonders, as Miss Abers, a tall, kindly teacher, gives out supplies for a hand-embroidery project.

"Always use a thimble," she cautions. She wears her dark-brown hair, sprinkled with silvery gray, high on her head in a bun. Her dress skims over the tops of her sturdy, high-buttoned shoes. Its beige serge material would have looked quite plain, except that Miss Abers has decorated the sides of its sleeves and its hemline with embroidered white daisies, with yellow centers on green stems, alternating with purple irises. Many girls "ooh" and "ahh" at her handiwork.

But Mollie is bored, bored, bored.

Each girl receives a white muslin napkin on which to embroider. It has a thin blue line drawing to show where to stitch a pattern of roses, leaves, and stems. The threads are in red, burgundy, and pink shades for the flowers, and light- and dark-green for the stems and leaves. Most girls eagerly begin cross-stitching rose petals before Miss Abers concludes her demonstration.

Mollie forgets the thimble, lackadaisically threads her needle with red thread, and sticks it listlessly through the fabric, where it stays while she gazes out the window.

I wish I were still in gym class, she thinks. *I love the gym. I could be practicing my new routine on the uneven parallel bars. The gymnastics contest is only a week away.*

Girls from the Academy's high school competed with other public high schools in Manhattan and the Bronx. After winning an earlier contest, Mollie became a minor celebrity at the Academy. On seeing her in school halls and the dormitory, acquaintances asked, "How's the champion doing?" Mollie would smile as if to say, "Aw, shucks," but beamed at the recognition.

Still looking out the window, Mollie notices the cascading, bright autumn leaves of a large maple tree. The breeze blows them about in a circular pattern. *So graceful; they could be dancing.*

Yes, dancing! Mollie loves dancing and wants to choreograph a dance as a gym project that would include eight other girls. She will call it the Rope Dance because she will hold a long rope and swirl it this way and that, creating the illusion that the rope controls the twirls of the dancers, who, as an ensemble, will make snake-like movements.

The dance will begin with all the girls lying in a chain of bodies on the stage floor in a pattern that looks like a long, writhing snake. As it concludes, Mollie will lie down flat on her stomach as the tail. She will raise her legs from the hip area to curve up from the floor, then move them from side to side as a snake would move its tail. *Good thing I'm loose-jointed.* She will begin at the performance's climax, and the others will join in to make a loud hissing sound.

"Mollie, are you having a hard time getting started?" Miss Abers asks softly. Startled, she snaps to attention. She is embarrassed by her next thought as she regards her teacher: *If Miss*

Abers were to loosen her bun, her long hair would be perfect: dark, wavy, and sleek enough to flow with the graceful movements of the lead snake dancer. The silver strands in her hair would add drama and sparkle.

"I'm sorry," Mollie apologizes. "I was just thinking about something." Her cheeks are red and feel warm. She collects herself and returns to her sewing task with such intensity that she pokes the needle into a finger anchoring the napkin. Mollie bites her tongue to avoid crying out. A drop of blood surfaces on her skin and then trickles down to stain the napkin. Miss Abers has already moved toward another student, her back to Mollie. Had she seen, Mollie thinks she would have said, "Uh-oh! Remember your thimble."

This is the last straw. I've got to get out of here.

There is a math class across the hall—all boys, except for Esther.

Lucky Esther has a mother to stick up for her. Mollie presses her finger to stop the bleeding. *But if Esther can be in a math class, why can't I? A dance choreographer needs to understand mathematics. And these girls will be thrilled to sew our costumes,* she realizes as she looks around the room.

Mollie takes a deep breath and squares her jaw. She places the napkin, needle, and thread on the table. While Miss Abers is bent over a girl's work, demonstrating a different stitch for the green stems, Mollie stands and tiptoes out of the room and into the mathematics classroom. The teacher is writing an algebra problem on the chalkboard with his back to the class. Mollie slips into a vacant seat in the last row, next to Esther, whose eyes widen on seeing her friend. Mollie puts an index finger over her lips. A couple of curious young male heads turn toward her, but she stares at the problem on the chalkboard, and they quickly do the same.

I like it here. Mollie's lips curve into a faint smile as she copies the problem into her notebook.

The "boys'" math class became a stepping stone for more academic courses and, eventually, higher education and a career my mother loved.

"So Marcia," she said, concluding her story, "when they saw how I took to math, they let me join Esther in the other academic classes. But I always liked gymnastics best. And dancing, of course."

"Granny Judson encouraged me every step of the way," my mother said. Gloria and I called Corinne Judson by that name, and my mother sometimes called her "my godmother."

"Corinne Judson formed a girls club, a group of twelve-year-olds from the Academy. She took us on outings and invited us for meals at her home." Granny Judson lived with her husband, Abe, in an apartment overlooking Central Park. Several of the girls, including my mother, became her lifelong friends. She hosted my parents' wedding in her apartment.

"Did I ever tell you how I got a college scholarship?" my mother asked. But we'd both run out of steam by then. She said, "I'll tell you about Uncle Louie and the scholarship committee some other time. It's quite a story."

My mother's gutsiness was her ticket out of misery. I was proud of her for going after what she wanted. Yet I was embarrassed, at thirteen, seeing her pirouette uninhibitedly from the kitchen to the living room, her black, filmy circle skirt flaring out from her sturdy hips and thighs. I was shy, too self-conscious to dance, and hadn't even watched *American Bandstand*. I never told my mother that her exuberant dancing mortified me.

I remember her talking at dinner sometimes about the snappy Alley Cat dance she invented and taught to her junior high gym students. She lined them up in rows to perform it; "Right leg in, out, switch to the left, keep going, wave arms . . ." That's how I pictured the dance, though I never saw it.

"They love the Alley Cat," she said.

28 – Mom's Mentor

My mother's letters were usually upbeat, a couple of pages, sometimes a short note on a scrap of paper written on a subway train or during a Broadway play's intermission. Today's letter was short and on light-blue stationery. I read it at my kitchen table:

Dear Marcia,

Sad news. Uncle Louie had a heart attack. He had been active until the end. I took today off to be at his funeral. A wonderful person. His memory will live on.

I love you,

Mom

"Uncle" Louie wasn't her uncle or mine. He was Louis Straus, a wealthy philanthropist. I vaguely remember visiting him with my mother at his elegant Manhattan apartment on Park Avenue and being surprised when the elevator opened right into his place.

An old photo of him rested on our Rockaway home's fireplace mantel. With his pinstriped suit, wire-rimmed eyeglasses, and a stalwart expression, he looked like the upright, prosperous citizen he was. His straight, dark hair was slicked back 1940's movie-star style. I'd heard about Uncle Louie all my life. I stared at the letter now, taking in the news.

I pictured my mother on a recent trip to see him, not knowing it would be the last time. I imagine she felt young riding the IRT subway train from Flatbush Avenue in Brooklyn, because she'd known Uncle Louie since her youth. The train's jerky, swaying motions jostled her. She thought of tidbits of good news to share with Louis. Sensing he wanted this, she tried to be upbeat with him.

When the train stopped at the Nevins Street station in downtown Brooklyn, my mother may have remembered going there with Gloria and me. We went to A&S and May's department stores. The last time she and I were there, she'd helped me pick out clothes for college: tailored wool skirts, a corduroy suit, and cotton blouses in rich shades of brown, green, and russet. Her newspaper might have fallen in her lap while she thought, *I would have felt in seventh heaven to have had those beautiful, new clothes, but I was lucky to go to college, thanks to Louis Straus.*

Mom and Louis Straus had an unlikely friendship. Twenty years her senior, he was born "with a silver spoon in his mouth," as the saying goes. He'd owned a seat on the New York Stock Exchange for decades. He stayed calm and afloat during the Great Depression of the 1930s, thanks to his conservative "never buy on margin" investment style.

They first met when my mother was seventeen and longed to go to college and have a career as a dancer. But there was a problem. She asked her good friend, Esther, to help.

They walked around the block on a warm spring day. Mollie needed to get the kinks out of her body and brain. The trees were turning green, and the air smelled of hope and promise. But she felt gloomy.

"Esther, I wish I could attend college on a scholarship. It's not fair. I want to be a dancer. But if I tell that to the scholarship committee, they won't give me a cent."

"And you should be a dancer. Your Rope Dance was amazing! The audience didn't know what hit them for a minute, and then: thunderous applause!"

"But, Esther, they don't want me to be a dancer," said Mollie, slowing her pace to her friend's less athletic one.

"But you *are* a dancer, Mollie. You were born to be one; it's all you want to do."

"Oh, I am, I am, and yes, it's all I want to do. But they won't help me become one because they think it's like being a—you know . . ."

Esther seemed confused, then a look of recognition came into her eyes. Neither of them would say *prostitute*; it skirted the edge of their vocabularies.

"Mollie, what will you do?"

"I don't know. My interview with the scholarship committee is in three days. I'll have to tell them something."

She couldn't say she wanted to be a dancer. She had to come up with something else for the scholarship committee. But what?

Mollie slept sporadically that night. When her mind returned to the applause for her Rope Dance, she felt a surge of gratitude for Miss Brummer. Dear Miss Brummer, her gym teacher, who helped make the Rope Dance a success. She was more than a teacher—she was a coach or friend. Still in her twenties, Miss Brummer wore bloomers like the girls in her gym classes—

A job like hers. I could teach what I love: gymnastics and dancing.

"A gym teacher," said Louie Straus, who headed the Hebrew Orphans Asylum's scholarship committee, after Mollie announced her new ambition. "That's terrific," he'd said, eyes twinkling. "The world wants people who can do things. And," he added, "a teaching job won't be vulnerable to shifts in the economy."

"Call me *Louie*, please, Mollie," he'd said after she'd earned her Master of Education degree. *Mr. Straus* makes me feel ancient."

During one visit, he surprised her by saying wistfully, "I should have married you, Mollie."

Of course, I never viewed him that way, she thought. *He lives in a different world*. Still, she'd felt complimented, even if an old bachelor's fantasy wasn't meant to be taken seriously.

Louie was right. I love teaching and feel wanted at school every day, Mollie thought as the train reached Manhattan. On that day of her last visit, my mother knew Louie would ask her about teaching and about Gloria and Marcia, as he always did during her visits. She would mention Marcia's talk at a big conference about alcoholism. She'd tell him Gloria was pregnant again and that her gym students loved the Alley Cat Dance. She could still hear Louie's words from long ago: *The world wants people who can do things.*

My mother wouldn't mention that the teachers might strike and wanted her to picket, but she felt torn. She didn't want anyone to get angry at her—the strikers would stop speaking to her if she didn't strike; the nonstrikers would resent her if she did. Louis was a Republican, so why would he want to know about a strike? My mother acted like she agreed with him when Louis talked about politics, although she voted for Democrats.

She recognized the doorman at the large stone apartment building. An elevator took her into Louie's two-story apartment, where a uniformed maid greeted her. Mollie was still awed by the high ceilings, Persian carpets, original oil paintings, and by Louis, who rose from his seat. The maid brought pastries and tea to the mahogany dining table.

"Hello, Mollie. It is so good to see you again," he said.

He's still vigorous at eighty, Mollie thought, noticing his straight posture and energetic stride as he approached her, and she extended a hand to meet his. A broad smile transformed his usually solemn face.

I imagine my mother doubted Louis Straus would have married her. But he had the right qualities for a surrogate father.

He championed her achievements, even if he couldn't give her unconditional love. What was *that*, anyway, she might have wondered, never having experienced it.

Year after year, well into middle age, my mother related to Louis as a cheerful, grateful orphanage girl, playing Annie to Daddy Warbucks.

And now Uncle Louie was gone. I'd thought of him for a long time as someone larger than life who would always be in my mother's life. Because I barely knew him, I felt more surprise than grief about his passing. I imagine my mother missed him deeply.

I put the note in my box of saved letters.

29 – Threatened with Exposure

1977. San Francisco General Hospital

Bruce Merton was right about the new, improved San Francisco General Hospital. It was sleek, modern, and seven stories high. Its large windows alternated with shiny, pale- and emerald-green panels that reflected the Mission District's sunlight.

The psych ward I worked on, 7C, was bright and airy. The nurses' station faced a large, open space with cream-colored walls. I often passed through its locked double doors to or from my office. At first, I spent much time observing patients in the common area, many of whom I found interesting.

Jackie was my favorite. She was back every few months, a bright-eyed, slim quasi-hippie in her early thirties with a sweet face. Her schizophrenia symptoms returned after she stopped taking Haldol because it blurred her concentration. Jackie wore her wheat-colored hair in braids and clothed herself in loose, floral dresses over long pants. Her style looked odd then but later became fashionable.

"I'm a vegetarian," she announced, pacing around the dayroom. "I don't want to hurt the poor animals." She often talked about her love for cats, dogs, birds, and other creatures.

Another patient asked her, "What about the poor plants?"

I enjoyed the bustling atmosphere and uninhibited talk of many patients. Occasionally, one physically attacked another or a staff member, seemingly unprovoked. When this happened, a cluster of staff, usually psych techs and nurses, shoved the offender against a wall or pushed him to the floor, then put him in a padded isolation room to calm down. The procedure struck me as both savage and needed, for lack of a better alternative.

Aside from one frightening exception, when a patient to whom I denied a pass tried to knock me down and a psych tech cut him off, I felt safe on the ward.

Safe among my colleagues too. They were respectful, a refreshing change from coworkers who harassed me at the alcoholism treatment center. If anyone knew about my psychiatric history, they didn't let on.

Like Jackie, many patients kept returning, a "revolving door" syndrome. Schizophrenia and manic-depression were the two most common diagnoses. After a few days on medication, their symptoms usually cleared up. Once discharged, many stopped taking their meds because they slowed them down or interfered with their thinking.

Not only did I tell patients it was crucial to continue their medication if they wanted to stay out of the hospital, but I told myself I must keep taking lithium.

I strove to get patients stabilized and discharged promptly. As I predicted at Booth Memorial, my experience as a psychiatric inpatient made me see things from both sides.

I sensed that my empathy for patients here was like the kind of understanding recovering alcoholics typically have for practicing ones. My colleagues respected my work, but I feared their esteem would plunge if I came out of the psychiatric closet.

My efforts to move patients out as soon as possible resulted in my having a heavier load than my colleagues. As soon as I discharged one patient, I would be assigned a new one, which meant I had to develop more treatment and discharge plans and complete more paperwork than other therapists.

Remembering that my menstrual periods had arrived just about the time of each of my three hospitalizations, I wondered if this happened to many of our female patients. I initiated a research project in which I interviewed newly admitted women. I found a possible correlation between the date they came to the ward and when their period arrived, but I needed to enlarge the study for more conclusive results. Before that could happen, though, my daily caseload on the ward increased because of some personnel shifts.

Consequently, I had to drop the Menses and Psychiatric Admissions study and no longer had time to serve on various committees. I was disappointed to give up these voluntary activities, which challenged me and balanced my routine clinical duties.

Something happened that almost blew my cover, if I had one, which, in retrospect, was hard to believe. One day, a new patient caught my attention as I went to the ward's conference room. He looked vaguely familiar.

"Hey!" he called out. "Don't I know you from somewhere?" I looked at him and felt a sinking feeling in my gut. "Langley Porter, that's it," he called out and laughed. "Langley Porter. Hey, how 'bout that?"

No one was in earshot. Wishing I could disappear, I looked at him blankly, like he was mistaken.

"Yeah! I remember you. Don't you remember me?" he smiled. Was he accusing or just being friendly? Too off-balance to know, I stood frozen in place.

"Ping-pong! I remember," he said loudly. "Don't you?"

"No," I lied, shrugging my shoulders and avoiding his eyes. I sensed he saw through me, and I rushed off.

I was relieved when they didn't assign Henry to my team. But I felt uneasy, like a potential blackmail victim, until his discharge.

Studiously, I avoided him, quivering inside, wondering, *Did he tell anyone?*

In time, I forgot about Henry—until he was readmitted. "Hi there," he said at that time. I heard, "I can ruin you."

I wanted to say, *please don't tell*, but I was still pretending I'd never seen him before. Then I saw his name on my list of patients on the large whiteboard that paired patients with their primary therapists. *No, no, no!*

I'd become friendly with Barbara, a psychology intern in her forties on a different team. I considered her mature and trustworthy. Hoping she wouldn't ask why, and with knots in my stomach, I told Barbara privately that I wasn't comfortable being Henry's therapist."

"I'll take him," she said, like it was no big deal.

"Thank you," I gasped, touched by her easy generosity.

I still wondered if Henry had revealed my secret. Could someone in a psychotic state exercise discretion? Had he relished saying: *She's as crazy as the rest of us?*

Did Barbara know? Did everyone?

After his discharge, I waited for the proverbial other shoe to drop, for the next time he'd show up on the ward. But I never saw him again.

30 – Intuitions and Intentions

1979. San Francisco, California

My breath caught in my throat when I saw an article on my desk: "Treatment of Mania in the Last Six Months of Pregnancy." Attached was a simple note, "FYI," from our ward chief, Dr. Ron Jablonski. I closed the door and wondered. Did he know my secret? Was he discreetly trying to be helpful?

I knew Ron wouldn't expose me. A Harvard graduate, he was intelligent, easygoing, and good-natured. Ron had a kind, sensitive face and soft, fluffy red hair. At thirty, he was married with a three-year-old son, yet he had an innocent aura.

Ron wouldn't have hurt a fly. But if he did know about me, who else might? What possessed him to give me this article if he hadn't heard about my diagnosis? It warned that psychotropic agents for treating manic-depressive illness could cause birth and postnatal difficulties. We hadn't seen any pregnant manic-depressive patients on the ward. I filed the article under *Lithium*.

Could Ron have known I'd begun thinking my biological clock was ticking at thirty-five?

Still numb toward men three years after ending it with Len, I hadn't felt optimistic about marrying. I didn't yearn for a baby, but I wanted to keep my options open.

I fantasized about having a baby without a husband, as some women did. At this point, I'd settled into my new condominium in Marin County and loved its views of Mount Tamalpais and San Francisco Bay. I swam in the condo's pool, soaked in the hot tub, and renewed my friendship with Betty, a friend from San Francisco's Child Welfare Department who now lived nearby.

"You're nesting," Eileen said as she saw my new furnishings. I'd stopped waiting for marriage to buy nice furniture, so she was right.

I was reading a book on my new, off-white Haitian cotton-covered couch one day, when my mother called. "Interesting news," she said. "You know Marge Reilley across the street?"

"No," I said. I hadn't kept track of new neighbors in Rockaway.

"Well, her seventeen-year-old daughter is pregnant. She's still in high school. Marge says she'll let her daughter and the baby live with her." Marge would care for the baby, and her daughter would finish high school. "Isn't that wonderful," gushed my mother. "If you want to do that too, you can move in here, and I'll help."

I was astonished. Before I'd ruled out motherhood on my own, my mother seemed to intuit what I was thinking. I had moved across the continent and cut her out of my life for a full year. After ending the estrangement, I stopped telling her about my social life. Yet, she seemed to read my mind about motherhood—and what else, I wondered.

Motherhood was far from my mind on the day I attended the American Psychiatric Association meeting in San Francisco. Instead, I was eager to gain more information about treatment for manic-depression, for my own sake and for some of my patients. At one session, the speaker said the therapeutic lithium level was between 0.6 and 1.2 mEq/L. How could that be correct? I wondered. I was doing fine on Dr. Folger's dosage after I mentioned drowsiness: 0.3 mEq/L—half the lowest recommended amount!

The speaker also noted that salt potentiates lithium, meaning one's diet should include it for lithium to be effective. That seemingly minor fact soon slipped from my mind.

I felt the urge to stand up in my dressed-for-success suit and announce: "Some people may not need to put so much lithium into their systems. I'm a living example, being maintained well with one, 300-milligram pill daily, not the standard three or four usually prescribed pills that increase risks of kidney damage and other harmful side effects."

But I sensed exposing myself would be professional suicide.

Jackie, the vegetarian quasi-hippie, continued to return to the ward. "Hello, Miss Fisch," she'd snarl at me, furious at being caged again. After they sedated her, Jackie became cheerful in a childlike way.

One time, when she'd been unmedicated and living on the streets of downtown San Francisco, she took a cane away from a blind man and hit him with it. The victim's caseworker decided to empower her client by bringing the incident to the criminal justice system. I had to explain to the judge why Jackie wasn't your ordinary battery committer and that anything could happen when she didn't take her medicine.

Jackie's husband and their five-year-old daughter lived a few hours away. When her husband visited her, I was impressed by what a normal, regular guy he seemed to be. Jackie must have been mentally healthier when they married. It wouldn't have been possible for them to live together if she had refused her medicine. "You don't know what it's like to take yucky pills," she told me accusingly.

I kept taking lithium.

But unlike her pills, mine gave me no side effects. Yet I remembered how Thorazine had kept me in a fog at Elmhurst. And Prolixin, prescribed at Booth Memorial, had turned me into a partial zombie.

I *did* know what it was like. *Both sides.*

Jane Yin, a twenty-three-year-old social work graduate student at the University of California, Berkeley, had been a San Francisco Chinatown gang member in her teens. You wouldn't guess this on seeing her petite size and her pretty face framed by long hair.

I'd supervised Jane's field placement at San Francisco General Hospital for nearly a year when she informed me about my life as she saw it. We sat at a table in the ward's large dayroom.

Jane impressed me early on when I observed her respond to a hefty male patient who tried to manipulate her. She didn't have to say a word; her facial expression and stance spoke silently to him: *Don't mess with me. I have your number*. He got the message.

Over time, Jane and I developed a mutually respectful, trusting relationship. So I felt okay that day as we relaxed at the table to lament that I was still single.

"Oh, Miss Fisch," she said. You don't want to get married. You like your life. You want to be an agency director."

I looked at her, astonished. Was she right? Lacking a steady man in my life at thirty-six, I busied myself honing my public speaking and leadership skills as a member of the Marin Toastmistress Club. I studied the *Dress for Success* book when all the ward's team leaders were male psychiatrists. When I started wearing my new, navy pinstripe or gray wool suit, patients directed comments and questions to me during our daily team meetings with therapists and patients as though I were the one in charge. Delighted, I would respond, glancing toward the psychiatrist in shirt sleeves, "Ask Dr. Miller."

Was Jane right? Part of me thought so. But another part quietly moved into a homemaker role when a new boyfriend came along. I'd start baking cookies and cooking entire meals instead of only a baked potato or avocado for dinner. When the relationship ended, I felt like less of a person.

"You may be right," I told Jane, only partially convinced.

Ron Jablonski, the ward chief, and Bruce Merton wrote glowing evaluations, praising me for doing more than my share of clinical and administrative work, my family therapy skills, and being a role model for colleagues and students.

Ron was also an Assistant Clinical Professor at the University of California School of Medicine in San Francisco. The school approved his recommendation for me to be given a clinical faculty position as a lecturer in recognition of my training psychiatry residents and medical students. This felt terrific.

I remembered my mother saying what Louis Straus, her recently deceased, lifelong friend, told her: "The world wants people who can do things." At San Francisco General, I felt valued for what I did.

Yet, I had become bored after my increased caseload swallowed up time I'd been able to devote to administrative and research activities. Perhaps I would have wanted to leave regardless after four years at the hospital. Like Jackie, I yearned to be free; in my case, free to enter a new direction in life.

31 – Learning about Judaism and Marriage

1982. Oakland, California

My intern at San Francisco General Hospital, Jane, was right. I wanted to run an agency. When I heard that a Jewish Family Service agency was looking for a new executive director, I applied and was hired.

I soon sensed I was in over my head.

The agency's primary focus had been therapy and counseling. Lorna was the agency's most experienced social worker. She mentored others, and staff and board members valued her. A relative of the board president had been one of her therapy clients.

The executive director who hired Lorna had been a friend of her father's. He and his successor tolerated her insubordination and other unprofessional behaviors for over two decades. People seemed to accept her lapses as though she were a family member.

Andrew Friedman, the executive vice president of the Jewish Federation that funded many of our agency's services, knew about Lorna. "Fire her," he advised before I started the job. "She'll be a thorn in your side, undermining and embarrassing you."

But fire someone I hadn't yet worked with? I'd never fired anyone or worked as an administrative supervisor with hire-fire authority. So I decided to wait and see. At first, Lorna was respectful to me, sometimes verging on obsequiousness. She said she was glad the agency had an executive director with clinical skills.

My first issue with her surfaced when she breached what should have been a professional boundary with one of her clients. I learned that from him because he was an old friend from the University of Michigan. He told me that Lorna complained during a session with him that our agency might have to stop offering long-term therapy. She knew the board wanted to free up staff time to serve the community with more short-term services.

I told Lorna that sharing her feelings about agency politics with a client was inappropriate. She agreed and apologized. But gradually, she showed the kinds of behaviors Andrew had warned me about. She came late for weekly staff meetings, ignored my requests to be on time, and undermined me in other subtle ways. My attempts to improve her usually resulted in short-term compliance. I appreciated her knowledge and experience and tried to ignore her faults while facing different challenges.

One concern was my lack of Jewish knowledge, which became an obstacle when I gave talks at synagogues and other organizations. "It's becoming embarrassing," Andrew said from across his desk. His face showed a pained expression on his delicate features when he said, "As executive director of Jewish Family Service, you're very visible. You go out into the community, and speak at synagogues and to Hadassah groups. You know *bubkes* about Judaism."

That wasn't totally true. I knew "bubkes" meant "nothing" in Yiddish. But it was true that I knew little about Sabbath observance and many other Jewish practices.

Andrew had a superb ability to make everyone feel like he was their best friend, which guaranteed his tenure as the Federation's executive vice president. He was fifty-eight, short, trim, balding, and sharp enough to outmaneuver anyone who might try to topple him from his politically sensitive position.

He served at the pleasure of the Federation's board of directors, generous donors who controlled its purse strings, voting annually on which agencies to grant money and how much. Mine, Jewish Family Service, was one of its largest grant recipients.

"So what?" I said to Andrew. "Is it such a big deal? I thought they hired me to lead the agency. Must I turn into a different person?"

"Look, Marcia, if you went to work in a foreign country, say Morocco or somewhere, wouldn't it behoove you to learn about the culture there?"

"Well . . ." He had me there.

"Whatever you do, say, what you know—and don't know—it reflects on your agency. You've put all this effort into rebuilding its reputation. You don't want to wreck it now by sounding ignorant about Judaism in public. Maybe you should take a class."

I felt like screaming. Already working two or three nights a week and fielding calls at home from my agency's board members on evenings and weekends, often about trifles, I didn't need more on my plate.

"I'll consider it," I mumbled, barely hiding my resentment.

"And by the way," Andrew added, like an afterthought, "You're getting a reputation for your skill in budgeting. You're one of the few agency directors who consistently keeps it in balance." He played me like a violin.

Back in my office, I dropped my head on my desk, wanting to erase what happened. Andrew was right. My lack of Jewish knowledge could hurt my agency.

When Andrew advised the agency's board of directors to hire me, my Jewish identity was mainly gastronomic. I briefly attended a Jewish after-school program at West End Temple in Rockaway when I was ten because a friend went there. I would have stayed away if I'd known how dangerous it was.

Each Wednesday afternoon, before the teacher arrived, students engaged in a knock-down, drag-out fight, boys against girls. They threw wooden chairs, ducked for cover, and overturned desks. The fact that no one got injured can be explained solely by Divine Providence, a concept unknown to me back then.

Although we pledged allegiance as one nation under *Him*, the only person in my family who mentioned G-d was my father, to say he didn't believe in Him. He'd rebelled at thirteen, refusing to have a Bar Mitzvah ceremony.

My mother told me she'd wanted to light Sabbath candles but feared upsetting my father. Occasionally she took me to Friday night services at West End Temple, a Reform synagogue, where she sometimes fell asleep, and I was bored. Our family ate lox and bagels and bacon and cheeseburgers.

After several Wednesday afternoons of learning to read Hebrew words without knowing their meanings, our teacher announced exciting news: new carpeting in the sanctuary! We were told not to bring in food or beverages. When we joined the other classes for a program, I felt queasy, maybe from something I ate. We trooped into the large sanctuary, almost tiptoeing on the plush, red carpet. As I entered our row of seats, I threw up.

"Whatever you want," said my mother when I came home and said I wanted to quit. Maybe she understood that my body said the school made me sick. I didn't go back.

So what if Andrew was right? I barely had time for a social life, and now he wanted me to learn about Judaism. Who was he to tell me what to do? Yet, he had a point.

I started attending Friday night services at the local Reform synagogue. I found solace and sociability there and liked the rabbi's uplifting sermons, the stunning stained-glass window high above the bimah, and the cantor singing a beautiful song about the world being a narrow bridge and yet we should not be afraid.

I felt moved when we chanted the "Shema" prayer, affirming the oneness of G-d. I found some prayers uplifting, and my eyes watered. Nothing was demanded of me. Unlike being at work or socializing, I liked this time to *be*.

At first, I went occasionally, then regularly, and became a dues-paying member. When the rabbi announced the formation of havurah (friendship) groups, I joined one. I liked the mix as we gathered at a large round table in the synagogue's social hall for the first time, along with other new havurah groups.

My group had four couples, two single men, and three single women. *This will be interesting*, I thought, *a chance to be with couples and maybe view good marriages. I had seen few over time.* One husband and wife looked in love after many years of marriage. I wanted to learn their secret, to move past my series of disappointing relationships.

I was dating again. Gil, who wasn't Jewish, was a tall, slim, friendly guy, two years older than I, and ready for marriage. We met at a singles ski race at the Homewood ski resort by Lake Tahoe.

Gil arranged for me to meet his parents. His mother was going to cook dinner in his apartment and bring everything. Before she arrived, four thick steaks were defrosting on the kitchen counter. "What's this for?" I asked Gil.

"Just in case," he said matter-of-factly. "You never know how things will work out. My mother's manic-depressive, you know."

Yes, you told me before, and your mother's been fine on lithium for over a decade. I won't tell you my diagnosis.

Gil's mother, whom I liked immediately, was petite and gray-haired with a sweet manner. She would have fit in easily at a Schrafft's restaurant in Manhattan. His father looked like an older gray-haired version of Gil, with some extra weight around the middle.

After saying how glad she was to meet me, his mother efficiently chopped, mixed, boiled, and sautéed one of the best meals I'd ever had: Garlic bread, Caesar salad, and a succulent casserole made with noodles, salmon, and a creamy sauce. She'd created the recipe and won a cooking contest with it a few years earlier.

I hoped her husband didn't sell her short, as Gil did.

She brought me a gift, a small, colorful, tropical bird barrette with an orange feather for a tail, zany and touching. I loved it.

But not her son. I tried but couldn't. My father understood when he took us to dinner. He was in San Francisco, sent to a trade show to represent the technology magazine he worked for. Later, I asked him, "So what do you think?"

"He seems nice enough, but do you have fun with him?"

Fun? An interesting concept. Hmm . . . No. "It seems like the fun ones don't want to get married, and those who do are boring."

"There's an obvious solution."

"Really? What?"

"Marry the boring one and have fun on the side."

I groaned inside. *Was he kidding? Like you did with Mom? And what about Ethel? I doubt she'd let you get away with it.*

At first, I thought Gil was fun. He had a dimpled smile and liked to put women, already wearing skis, on his shoulders and ski down a hill, piggyback. The first time I did it with him, I "whee'd" and giggled. After a while, I noticed him doing this with women from his ski club like a friendly tradition, a ritual with no spontaneity. With that awareness, I said "no thanks" when he offered me a ride until he stopped asking.

After Gil started hinting about giving me an engagement ring, I found fault with him left and right. One time he told me, "I'd like to treat the folks (his parents—that's how he talked) to a trip to Hawaii. They always wanted to go, but I can't afford it yet." We were at Tadich Grill, one of his frequent haunts. It reeked of Old San Francisco, with its dark, wood paneling, solidly constructed booths, and large steak and seafood platters.

"I don't get it. You own a successful business, but you don't save. You eat out all the time. Why don't you buy a used car like I do, instead of leasing a new one? I earn less than you, and I save."

One of the things I found endearing about Gil at first was how he'd get the same breakfast every day at this trendy place near where he lived. I watched the waiter bring him coffee and a pastry without waiting for him to order. *But eventually*, I thought, *what a waste of money. He could make the same thing at home.*

"I write it off as a business expense."

"But you don't save enough to pay for a trip to Hawaii."

"Oh, I will. I have to get organized. Just a matter of time."

But what turned me off most was Gil's dirty fighting. I confided in him earlier that Eileen had criticized me for being "difficult." Later, Gil used this against me during an argument: "Even your friends say you're hard to get along with," he said. *If I married him, he'd hold my manic-depression diagnosis over my head like a club.*

When I criticized Gil to Dr. Folger during a therapy session, he said, "This is San Francisco. One hundred women would be glad to marry him."

Not me. Gil finally had enough of my carping and cooled off. "I'm feeling put off by all your complaints," he said.

Okay, I thought. *This is how I break off relationships. Instead of ending them myself, I provoke the man to move on.*

The fact that Gil wasn't Jewish hadn't seemed relevant. My mother's advice long ago to "marry someone from our faith" hadn't impressed me consciously. I liked my non-Jewish aunts, whom my father's two brothers had married. Still, my paternal grandmother had asked about a guy I dated in my teens, "Is he Jewish?"

The Jewish couples in the havurah group looked well-matched and happy. Our group met monthly. We did things like read and discuss a book on a Jewish topic, went on outings, or gathered in a home for a potluck meal. I watched my favorite couple, fascinated. They met in college, married after graduating, and were about my age. He was tall, dark, and handsome. She was pretty, with faint freckles on her face and shoulder-length, brown hair. Their daughters in middle school looked like her.

When I admired their newly remodeled kitchen, she said, "We refurnished his den a couple of years ago. This time it was my turn; I got my kitchen."

Wow, they take turns.

Another happy-looking couple in the group came to the synagogue regularly on Friday nights. I was surprised when this husband quipped during the socializing time following the services: "Being married means having to eat sh-t."

Was he serious? I think he meant you have to do things for the other person you might not want to do.

Elliot, a married colleague at the Child Welfare Department, said about his relationship with his wife, "Sometimes I want to say something critical, but I don't. I'd rather stay married."

I was unconsciously picking up marriage mentors, though it took time for me to apply their teachings.

Knowing I wanted marriage, I signed up for a new-age, four-session class called "How to Find Your Soulmate." The teacher was a young, single woman who hadn't found hers.

32 – "How to Find Your Soulmate"

1984. Oakland and San Rafael, California

I continued taking lithium and stayed balanced while holding the demanding executive director job. I prepared budgets, wrote grants, collaborated with board members, and supervised staff. The two groups often had conflicting expectations, which I found stressful. Yet I liked the bragging rights and was proud to say I was an executive director.

I started taking Hebrew classes and learning more about Judaism. Until much later, I had no idea where the knowledge would take me.

At one staff meeting, Lorna said: "People suffer when disconnected from their Judaism. They need anchors to ground them, or it's like they float in space." Her words touched me; I sensed she was right.

One Sunday, I was at a health food store in Corte Madera. Among the many alternative healing books shelved near a display of crystals in a glass case, one about preventing premenstrual syndrome caught my eye.

I often felt heavy and sluggish before my period arrived. I took the book to a small table and skimmed through it, picking up on its recommendation to reduce salt intake.

Great idea, I thought, *and easy to implement*. I left the store and immediately eliminated salt from my diet. One problem: I forgot salt potentiates lithium; it needs salt to be effective.

On my second salt-free day, a Tuesday, I attended the last "How to Find Your Soul Mate" class session. The teacher was Lara, a petite woman with delicate features and short blond hair. She was in her late twenties and had an innocent aura.

Nearly forty and without a prospective husband, I was willing to overlook Lara's lack of counseling credentials. I wanted to believe her statement: "Each of us has a soulmate waiting to appear in our lives; we just need to get ready."

I hung on to her words like a lifeline. Six of us, men and women, all previously strangers, sat on cushions on the living room floor of her apartment.

Tonight Lara taught us to chant sounds while imagining ourselves filled with color. "Close your eyes and imagine green coming down and through your body, staying inside and all around you. Breathe in and out slowly." I pictured fresh-cut grass I walked through on an open field. I could smell it. I felt green swirl and surge through my body. Mm. "Now, on the exhale, chant, 'oooh.'" Lara's voice was calm and reassuring.

"Oooh," we sang in unison.

"Again, but draw it out. All together now."

"Oooooooooh."

"Much better. Now imagine blue coming into the top of your head and moving down little by little through every part of your body." A blue tropical sea. Blue sky.

I saw it and let it surround and enter me.

"Good. Now chant: 'Aaaah.'"

And so it went. Yellow was amazing. I felt the warmth of the sun coursing through my veins. "Eeeeh."

"Now visualize yourself as already having found your soulmate. Keep breathing in and out, in and out. When you feel relaxed, think about what will go wrong in this relationship.

Ask yourself, 'What am I afraid of?' Let your mind drift until you have an answer. You may want to share it with the group."

I relaxed at first as I breathed in and out, but as some thoughts seeped in, I forgot to breathe, and my chest tightened. *I want a baby. But I'm scared. My mother's mother—Yetta. Look what happened to her. I'll end up like her. She probably thought Morris was her soulmate. My husband will take off as he did. Leave me with a new baby. I'll crack up like my grandmother— locked up for life.*

I began to tremble. Lara noticed. "Marcia, do you want to tell us what's come up for you?"

"I want to have a baby, but I'm afraid . . ." My voice was shaking. I looked at the others, watching me intently. "I'm afraid I'll go crazy like my grandmother." I collapsed into a heap, crying.

"Keep breathing; breathe it out," Lara said tenderly. "Close your eyes and think of yellow again. Keep breathing slowly, in and out. Chant 'Ohhhh,' and drag it way out."

"Ohhhh." I forced myself to sit up again, but it wasn't working. I was still quaking.

"Keep breathing and listen to my voice." Calmly, she said, "You will have a baby and be okay. Repeat after me: 'I, Marcia, will be a mother, and I will be okay.'"

"I, Marcia, will be a mother, and I will be okay."

Lara sensed I wasn't convinced. "I want you to chant again, but this time surrender to the yellow; let it engulf you. Then say 'Ohhhh.'"

I closed my eyes again, let the sun's warmth surround me, and felt a tingling sensation up and down my chest and excitement in my stomach. I whispered: "I will have a baby, and I will be okay." I pictured myself holding my baby. My eyes moistened, and I tingled, alive with joy. I smiled. "Ohhhh."

"Do this every day until you have found your soulmate. And believe me, Marcia—and everyone—it will happen to you. It has already happened to me!"

We looked at her questioningly. "I met him last week and have seen him three times. We talk on the phone every night."

A few others talked about their fears and breathed them out. We agreed to keep doing the exercises independently, as this was the last class. Lara said, "Feel free to call me if anything comes up that you want to discuss."

The next day I was panicky. I thought it had something to do with the energy Lara had opened up in me, maybe too much too soon and nowhere to take it. I phoned her that night, sitting on my couch and clutching Red Riding Hood. We talked on and on but seemed to get nowhere.

"Something feels wrong with me. I feel agitated and jumpy, and it's hard to concentrate. I think something got stirred up in me in your class, so I hoped you could help—"

"You will be fine. I know trust is hard for you, but you can trust me."

"But I'm so scared. And it's hard to trust. I've been hurt before. Besides, I didn't tell you something about myself in class when I said I was afraid of going crazy. It's a secret; people shamed and treated me differently once they knew. I don't know whether it's too heavy for you to handle, but it relates to what I said about my grandmother and all—"

"It's okay. I can hear anything. I don't judge."

"I've been hospitalized in a psychiatric ward three times." I breathed in and out deeply, relieved to trust her with my secret. I waited for acknowledgment, even an "um-hmm," but there was silence. "I'm okay now, have been for over eight years, but what with what happened to my grandmother—"

"You will be fine," Lara said, as though trying to sound confident. Did she now view me as too messed up for her to tackle? "You need to believe in yourself and keep doing the exercises." She didn't sound as though she believed in me. Did she know what she was doing?

"But—"

"I'm really sorry, but I need to go. I have no boundaries. I talk to whoever calls me. I'm under a lot of stress now. My new boyfriend broke our Saturday night date and hasn't called since and—"

When I hung up the phone, I sensed Lara, the lifeline I'd been hanging on to, was a sinking ship.

33 – Salt-Free Diet's Effects

1985. Greenbrae, California

On my fourth salt-free day, I went through the motions at work but felt detached. At our staff meeting, I decided to help a social worker who needed some loosening up. While she and others looked on horrified, I explained that she would be much happier if she learned to have orgasms.

At that night's board meeting, I cracked jokes and stared at the banana I was eating instead of being alert to every nuance, as I usually tried to be. A board member I'd recruited, a married woman a few years younger than I, caught my eyes and smiled incredulously.

The meeting lasted past eleven p.m. Driving home on Route 80 through Berkeley towards the San Rafael turnoff, an eerie, other-worldly feeling overcame me. The cars rushed in multiple lanes through the black night in packs. The groups were far in front of and behind my car, leaving a vast space around me. I felt frightened by the odd configuration that set me alone on the freeway and sensed a message for me. But what?

I steadied myself and rode it out.

I felt oddly disconnected from the world when I arrived home, as though my physical self were null. I gave no thought to eating or taking the lithium. I turned off the lights and lay down. My thoughts kept racing, and I was awake all night.

The next day my mind worked overtime, shifting from one association to another while I sat on my couch. I thought I'd write them down, keep them alive, and propelled myself to my desk. On a fresh sheet of paper, I wrote:

Marriage   carriage   love   forever
fear   fair fare   no fear   risk   risky frisky
hear   hear you   hear me   hare   hair
love   today   tomorrow   always forever
love you   love mealways mine   yours   forever

Back on the couch, I held the paper in my lap and looked at my words. *Brilliant,* I thought. My gold ring caught my eye. *A wedding band.*

Sunlight filtered through my window's sheer curtain, accenting my ring's softly contoured tiny hills and valleys. I stared at the play of light and shadow on its surface, thinking, *not married; I'm not married.* I twirled the ring around, and then anxiety struck me. I yanked it off and placed it on my "wedding band" finger. *Now I'm married.*

"Married," I said out loud. *Married.* I felt relieved and happy. *Soon. Very soon. It's about to happen.*

I moved the ring up and down on my "married" finger, enjoying its smooth coolness on my skin. I stroked its wavy exterior, then stopped and jerked my head up. My breathing stopped, and my chest felt tight. *Married?* I screwed up my face. *No.* I moved the ring back to its usual finger. *Single.* I looked at it triumphantly but soon again felt a shortness of breath. I shook my head, switched it back to my left hand's finger, and said, "Married." But a few seconds later, I was "single" again.

I shifted the ring back and forth between the two fingers more quickly. "Married … single … married … single … married."

At last, I grabbed the ring and threw it in an arc; it landed sound-lessly near the typewriter on the plush, yellow carpet.

I ignored it and walked toward the shelves behind my din-ing table. Among the knickknacks was a framed photograph of an ex-boyfriend named Art. *He loves me; he loves me not; he loves me; he loves me not. He loves me!* We had stopped seeing each other over six months ago, but I knew now that he loved me and wanted to marry me. I melted as I looked at the image of his smiling face.

I picked up the photo and kissed his glass-covered lips. I felt tender and happy. *You've known and been waiting for me to catch up with you all along. Finally, I have. We'll be together forever. I can feel your thoughts. We haven't talked in months, but you've communicated telepathically. Now I hear you loud and clear.*

We'll have a big wedding, a Jewish wedding, at Rodef Shalom. You're not Jewish, but you don't mind. Rabbi Barenbaum will offi-ciate. Finally, I'm ready. I can feel your energy. You're telling me even though you are not here, we are so connected, and this is it. We are getting married, and it will be wonderful. Yes, Rabbi Barenbaum will marry us, and it will be forever.

Forever? I started shaking. *Something feels wrong.* I returned the photo to the shelf and looked at it again critically. I saw some-thing different in the face, something I did not like, a face pre-tending to belong to a good person. *I don't trust you. You were married before and didn't stick it out—got divorced. No! I don't want to marry you.*

I put the photograph face down, not wanting to see it. *You want to use me. You've got a foot out the door already. I know.* I grabbed the photo and threw it at the wall. The glass cracked, a satisfying sound. For a moment, I felt relieved. *A narrow escape. But what now?*

"Ohhhh," I moaned, feeling lost and crumpled on the couch.
I don't care about him . . . but I'm so lonely.
I'm scared.

I phoned Betty. We'd been close friends since meeting as coworkers at San Francisco's Child Welfare Department.

"I'm glad you're home. Can you come over?"

"Marcia? Is that you?"

"I'm . . . I'm scared. I don't want to be alone."

"You sound . . . different."

"I don't know how to explain it, but I'm so nervous—"

"Have you had anything to eat?"

"I don't remember. Not for a while, though. Do you think I should?"

"I'll be right over."

"I'm so scared—"

"I'm coming."

She's coming!

She's right, I thought after we hung up. *I should eat. Something easy.* I took a box of instant hummus, poured the powder into a bowl, and mixed in water. It tasted like talcum powder. *Yuck.*

Betty arrived; her face looked tight and worried. She joined me at the table.

"You're eating. That's good."

"I can't eat it. It's awful."

"I think you need to eat *something*. Do you want something different?"

"Taste it, see what you think." I got some carrots to dip into it. She tried it.

"Mm, tastes okay to me."

I tried it again. "It tastes good now. It's because you're here. A friend makes all the difference." Another insight. I was amazed that the hummus was perfectly edible.

"It's fine. I'm feeling better already. You were right. I needed to eat. I'll be okay."

"Are you sure? I'm concerned—"

"I'm so glad you came. I'm okay now. I want to rest." I felt so relaxed with her there that I expected to be able to sleep as soon as she left.

"Okay, you probably need to sleep too. I'll call you later to see how you're doing."

But when she called later, I screamed, "I'm so scared! No one can help me. I don't know what to do." I hung up on her. She called back a couple of times, and I slammed down the receiver each time.

In a few minutes, I heard a loud knocking on my front door. "POLICE. OPEN UP."

I opened the door to two tall police officers in uniform. One was dark-haired with a Mediterranean complexion; the other was blond. "Hello," said the fair one as both entered. They stood a few feet apart near my dining table. They looked pleasant and young, maybe twenty-five. Handsome men.

"We want you to come with us," said his companion.

"I know what you want. You want to f— me, right?" I looked at him teasingly, then at the other. "You too, right?" He looked as though he might blush.

They both smiled in a good-natured, boy-next-door way. I trusted them—strapping young men. I didn't protest as they handcuffed my wrists and took me to their squad car.

I was in the psychiatric unit of Ross General Hospital for three days, long enough to stabilize my lithium level. The milieu there was friendly and respectful. When I returned to work, I said I'd had a cold. I doubt anyone believed me because my manic episode had begun there.

Before my salt-free experiment, I'd begun a formal disciplinary process toward Lorna. An applicant for the agency's secretarial position was present at a staff meeting. She would be working with all of us, so I wanted the staff's input before hiring. Lorna defiantly embarrassed me in front of everyone. She said, "I don't know why you have her here now with all of us."

This insubordination was the last straw for me. I wrote a memo warning her of "further consequences" should her disrespectful behavior continue. After receiving it, she resigned. She wrote a letter to the board and staff members, slandering me by falsely claiming I'd fired her.

Lorna had a loyal following of board and staff members. A formerly supportive member said she feared I'd fire her next. The social worker I'd humiliated in my manic state during a staff meeting glared at me and refused to speak to me. In retrospect, I couldn't blame her. I'd told her in front of the others to loosen up and have orgasms.

No one at work mentioned my bizarre behavior. I felt too much shame to bring it up myself. It seemed like we had a pact to avoid mentioning my manic episode.

I was soon asked to resign because the board wanted to move the agency in a new direction. It was true that they desired a shift away from therapy and into more concrete services to offer to more people. But I never learned the true reason why I was let go. Was it because I'd lost the trust of staff and board members for "firing" Lorna? Or because I'd been psychotic at work, including during a staff meeting?

I wonder now what would have happened if people viewed psychosis not as shameful but more like other medical conditions requiring treatment and sometimes hospitalization. Would the outcome have been different had I explained about lithium and my salt-free experiment?

The board had voted for a substantial raise for me a year earlier to recognize my achievements. I'd never been fired before. I felt awful. As many firings are, though, it was a blessing in disguise.

34 – Recognizing My Pattern

1985. San Francisco and Rockaway

Leaving my job at the family service agency allowed me to try something new. I started a business, Creative Marketing Solutions, selling promotional gifts, usually imprinted or engraved with a company's logo or message. I enjoyed meeting prospects, talking to factory reps, and networking.

Also, I finally had time and energy again for a personal life. At forty, I sensed that my still-single status was not due to a scarcity of marriageable men. Former boyfriends were marrying. Why had Len, the lawyer, chosen to wed a divorced school teacher with two children instead of me? What had been so wrong with Gil? Even if he did refer to his bride as "the wife," she looked happy when I ran into them at an apres-ski lodge.

Wait a minute! I'd ended those relationships because I didn't trust Len to be faithful or Gil to respect and accept me over time. I was diagnosed manic-depressive like his mother, an award-winning cook whom he didn't trust to make dinner. Besides, my father noticed that Gil wasn't fun.

But I'd also dated men who were mensches. They no longer appealed to me when they signaled interest in committing; I let them go too. They also found willing marriage partners; not all the men I dated were marriage-averse.

When my friends Amy and Michael came to see me when I visited Rockaway, we walked to the beach. Before cooling off in the ocean, Amy and I lay face-down on a blanket to soak up the late summer sun's rays. Michael sat cross-legged, gazing toward the horizon.

"How's your social life these days?" Amy asked, raising her torso to face me. I sat up, about to start my usual spiel, but Michael beat me to it in perfect parody:

"There's this guy, and you like him a lot, but when you want to get serious, he takes off," he said in a faintly mocking tone. He smiled good-naturedly, then looked at me squarely.

I stared at him, incredulous. "Am I that boring and predictable?"

"Amy shows me your letters," he said with a shrug, dusting the sand off his legs. I liked Michael but might not have written as much about my romantic life if I'd known he read my letters.

My pattern was probably obvious to many who had heard me lament over one failed relationship after another. But I'd been blind to it.

I probably hadn't told Amy about the guys I drove away with indifference or criticism. The noncommittal types were more fun and engaging. I thought their attention meant something.

My eyes drifted to a cluster of children shoveling sand into pails. They dumped them upside-down and gradually constructed a large, ornate castle.

"I'm so lucky I married Amy," Michael said.

Amy's warm smile, kind, calm manner, and quiet intelligence made me grateful for her friendship. We first met in our seventh-grade classroom, half a mile from our spot on this beach. Amy's personality complemented his and mine, too. He and I were more tightly strung; Amy balanced us.

Michael said, "According to my former therapist, there are six F's in marriage: food, fondness, fun, fighting, f---ing, and futility."

"Michael!" Amy protested, laughing.

Michael pretended to ignore her, yawning exaggeratedly. "I think I'll take a nap," he said. When he flopped face down on the blanket, I sensed he was hiding a grin.

Wow, I thought, trying silently to memorize the "six F's." How different from the romantic novels and movies that tout endless bliss. Michael and Amy had a good marriage that must have included conflicts and feelings of futility.

As a couples and family therapist, I knew people could have healthy marriages with problems. But I wasn't applying this knowledge in my personal life. I unconsciously believed that a good marriage resembled the effortless-happily-ever-after fairy-tale idea.

The tide was coming in as we shook the sand from our blanket and prepared to leave. The children had disappeared, leaving the sandcastle they had built several feet from the shore. The waves came closer and closer until they splashed over it. Gradually, they washed it away until nothing remained.

I decided to get therapy to help move past what kept me from marrying. A few weeks before leaving my executive director job, I asked a colleague from another agency to recommend someone. I wanted a Jewish male therapist who was still married to his original wife and had successfully raised children.

"The only one I suggest is Dr. Posner," he said. "He used to consult here. I think he's very good."

"He's Jewish?" I supposed I'd be better off with a Jewish husband, all things equal. Why not choose a therapist who was a real-life example of what I wanted?

"Yes."

"Married?" I wanted someone who knew how to do it.

"Yes."

"To his original wife?" A man who didn't leave.

"Yes!"

"Has he successfully raised children?" I still hoped to have a child. Did I want a role model for parenting? Or was I looking for a daddy? Maybe both?

"And how! He is the father of five, all adults now."

Yes! Yes! Yes!

I sensed my colleague liked Dr. Posner, not just as a therapist but as a person. "By the way," he added, "he sees adults, but his specialty is *child* psychiatry."

I didn't mind at all.

35 – Finding a Therapist

When I phoned Dr. Posner, I said I was interviewing several therapists before choosing one and wanted therapy to help me get married. I liked his calm, deep voice and his asking nothing of me except, "Would you like to schedule an appointment?"

Dr. Posner's office was on the second floor of a three-story office off Ashby Avenue in Berkeley.

Ten years earlier, when I told my mother I was seeing a therapist, Alan, she said, "Too much analysis leads to paralysis." She added, "They always blame the mother."

My second therapist was the closest anyone came to blaming her. Dr. Folger had said, tongue in cheek, "Don't let her give you that orphanage crap."

Dr. Posner had curly gray hair, a mustache, and a comfortably plump face and body. He looked to be in his late fifties. He introduced himself in the waiting room, then gestured me through a short hallway, past a kitchenette with a coffee maker, and into his office. It felt homey.

His upholstered chair looked well used. Near it, I was surprised to notice what I'd viewed only in movies, a psychoanalyst's couch on which a patient reclines, free associates, and recalls long-dormant memories. A stack of journals, with *Child Psychiatry* on top, rested on a small wooden table.

From my seat across from Dr. Posner, I thought his slightly rumpled tweed sports jacket, worn over a white turtleneck, made him look like a college professor who preferred comfort over style.

"How can I help you?" he asked.

I noticed his neck making small, involuntary movements, like tics or spasms, which I tried to ignore. "I want to get married, have wanted to for a long time, but whenever it seems like it might get close, I get critical of the man, find a 'wart' and reject him."

Dr. Posner's head was still now. His face looked soft, almost tender. He nodded for me to continue. *Has he had much experience working with adults?* I wondered, but the couch was probably for adults.

"I stop seeing the man if he wants marriage. If he doesn't, I become obsessed with wanting more commitment from him. I go for those who want a casual relationship until I can no longer fool myself into thinking they want more. Then I either give up or scare them away by demanding more. I spend some time mourning them, then find someone else. I've been in this pattern for a long time. But I'm forty now and want a husband, maybe a baby, " I looked at him, waiting for a response.

"I'm listening."

"Does this sound like something you can help me with?"

He paused before answering while I stared at the maroon carpet.

"It's an appropriate subject for therapy to get past a self-defeating pattern. It takes a combination," he said, so quietly I had to listen intently to hear, "of will on your part and time."

"How long would I need to come?"

"There is no way to predict this, but at least a year, probably longer. The process is likely to go faster if you come in more often."

"You mean it could be years?" It was hard to fathom. My previous therapies had sessions once a week and lasted a few months.

Dr. Posner nodded.

"Once a week, probably," I said. *This would be expensive. But if I could see someone who would help me for as long as it took to reach my goal* . . . "I'm not sure who I'll choose as my therapist; I'm looking into different possibilities."

"A decision you will be making," he said. I liked his calmness. Then, he did it again—his head moved like those bobbing heads on figurines of animals or famous baseball players seen through some cars' rear windows.

I said, "I'm noticing how your head is moving, bobbing up and down. It's a little distracting." I felt guilty and feared hurting his feelings.

In his quiet, deep voice, he said, "You have found my wart."

Ohhh! And you *have found mine.* My breath caught in my throat.

As I took out my checkbook to pay, Dr. Posner again astonished me. "There will be no charge," he said. "You are shopping."

36 – Adopting a Dog, Seeing Jackie

1985. Berkeley, California

"I've always wanted a dog," I said wistfully to Dr. Posner. Today, he wore a comfortable-looking brown corduroy jacket, a light blue shirt, and a plain tie. I hoped he'd tell me I could handle a dog. But after several sessions, I knew he wanted me to trust myself.

Dr. Posner looked more like a dog lover than a cat fan. I could see him walking a dog in the Berkeley Hills—home to many successful intellectual types—perhaps throwing a ball to a Golden Retriever in a park.

"But I don't know. I've never taken care of a dog." We had two during my childhood, but there were problems. The first one, Tippy, ran away. Our other one, Candy, was a sweet but lonely puppy, and she acted out destructively.

While her humans were at work or school one day, her sharp little teeth chewed the valance of our new couch. I came home from school to see my mother kneeling, pushing a needle through the couch's thick tweed fabric. Barely looking up, she said, "I must finish fixing this before your father gets home. Don't tell him."

Dad had threatened to give Candy away if she kept destroying things. While Mom sewed frantically, Candy sat contentedly by the antique spinning wheel next to the brick fireplace. Gloria and I loved the little dog and kept Mom's secret.

We had to give up Candy, anyway. She'd strained at her leash and bit two neighbors within a couple of weeks. Both made official complaints. The animal control officer said, "One more time, and she'll be taken to the pound." I was nine and didn't know what "pound" meant, but I wanted to keep her. But she bit someone else and was taken away. No one talked about what probably happened to her.

Like people lacking enough nurturing, dogs develop frustration that builds until it eats away at their insides or explodes outwards, assaulting furniture or living beings. After several years of a loveless marriage, my mother developed an ulcer. My father expressed his marital unhappiness by criticizing and straying.

"A dog is a big responsibility," I said as Dr. Posner looked on. "I've always wanted one, but how do I know if I'll be able to take care of it?" I'd learned not to expect him to give advice. Usually, when I asked what to do, he'd say, "Keep talking."

"I'm afraid I won't be able to handle a dog."

He listened expressionlessly, his head bobbing, which I was used to by then. I didn't know if the movement was a nervous habit or resulted from a physical problem. (Years later, I learned he'd had surgery for a back injury that may have caused it.)

"I've never had to take care of anybody or anything. I even forget to water the plants friends gave me as housewarming gifts. But now that I've stopped working, this would be a good time since I'm home often. But it's scary."

Dr. Posner scratched his head. "It is ludicrous," he said, "to think you can't care for a dog."

Still nervous about adopting a puppy, I went to San Francisco's animal shelter and told myself I was just looking. A cute, sleepy-looking, caged puppy perked up on seeing me and wagged her tail. I liked her.

A young volunteer opened her cage and took us outside to a grassy, enclosed area. She was a white mixed-breed terrier with tan markings. He said she wasn't likely to grow beyond a small to medium size.

As I watched her explore the area, the man offered to put her on my lap. Once she was there, I wanted to keep her. Yet, as I told him, "I'm not sure I can take care of a dog."

The man said, "I'm a hypnotist. I know you'll do fine. And you can bring her back within two weeks if you want."

A hypnotist? Really? Regardless, his assurance boosted me. I left carrying the puppy outside in a sturdy cardboard carton with handles they gave me. It had round breathing holes on its sides.

A voice called out on the sidewalk near my car, "Miss Fisch!"

It was Jackie, the animal-loving vegetarian frequently admitted to San Francisco General's psych ward, where I was her therapist. She wore a long, flower-print dress that swayed in the breeze, revealing jeans underneath.

"Can I see?" Jackie asked excitedly, her eyes glued to the box. She bent down to look through the holes. "Oh, soooo cute. Adorable, you little darling." She was eyeball to eyeball with the puppy, sounding like a little girl. "Precious, so sweet," she cooed, then dangled one of her long wheat-colored braids before a hole. She blew a kiss to the puppy, then turned to me. "Just adorable." She was radiant.

Of all the people to run into here, I thought, wonderstruck. But it made sense, with all her talk on the ward about loving animals, that she'd hang out here. I'd never thought much about how revolving-door patients lived between hospitalizations. Outside, Jackie looked like anybody in San Francisco with its tolerance for nonconformists and alternative lifestyles.

I couldn't have been happier to see her. I felt uplifted and confident about owning a dog. This was my first time seeing a former patient outside the hospital. *A good sign*, I thought, carefully placing the carton in my Cressida's passenger seat. I drove my puppy home and named her Amie.

Amie—named after my friend Amy—and I got along well. Her company fulfilled me. During her teething phase, when she destroyed one of my navy-blue, high-heeled shoes, I still loved her.

Amie, wearing her award medal
after winning a race.

37 – Ending the Game

1987. Greenbrae, California

Imet Rick in July at a Jewish singles hiking club gathering at the Pacific Heights apartment of Roberta, a tall, attractive woman whom I then met for the first time. Thirty of us were there, preparing for a weekend camping trip to Yosemite National Park. I felt young and perky in a short cotton dress with a ruffle at the knee.

At first, I barely noticed Rick. He'd been one of many people I'd talked with briefly that evening, and I vaguely recall him introducing himself to me. A clean, average-looking guy, Rick had small blue eyes behind glasses. Thin strands of brown hair were combed over his bald spot. Pale freckles dotted a face that looked like it should stay out of the sun.

Later at Yosemite, I saw Rick at twilight outside a small convenience store. I felt grimy, having just returned from an "easy" hike, seven miles, much of which was uphill. I longed for a shower and a nap.

"Hi, Marcia," Rick said brightly, "How was your day?" He looked freshly scrubbed, and his cotton jacket hadn't yet accumulated the dust that the breezes blew everywhere. He mentioned his grueling twelve-mile hike. Maybe it was pine fragrance filling the air. Or perhaps my resistance had weakened with the high altitude and post-hike fatigue. But I saw something sweet and charming in Rick, especially when his eyes brightened as they met mine and his face softened into a smile.

Later that evening, he joined me at the campfire, where the group conversed in quiet clusters. Roberta stared at the flames from a log on the other side of a big fire, cuddled close to her fiancé, a handsome astronomer she'd met hiking a few months before. *She's lucky*, I thought, barely allowing myself to long for what she had.

Bundled up for the cold, Rick and I sat on a thick log and played Boggle, a word game at which no one had previously beaten me, an English major. Bested by him, a computer program analyst, I must have looked flustered. "I'm sorry. It was an accident," he smiled sweetly. "It won't happen again, I promise." Tongue-tied and warm, though not from the fire, I looked at his gentle face, then down at my mittens.

We left the campfire and took a circuitous route back to my tent cabin. We talked about art, literature, and of course, nature. I told Rick how the mist around Yosemite's waterfalls reminded me of the diaphanous seascapes by my then-favorite artist, William Turner. I shivered in the cool night air, and he wrapped his arm around my shoulders. He said, "You're beautiful."

Rick arrived for our first date with a gift, Andrew Wilton's book, *Turner and the Sublime*. We played tennis that afternoon without keeping score; he knew not to after Boggle. The asphalt beneath my feet grounded my giddiness.

Back at my place, I struggled to open a juice bottle's twist-off lid before handing it to Rick. We took Amie for a walk along a nearby path by a creek. Other dog walkers, joggers, bicyclists, and occasional roller skaters were around. Rick held Amie's leash while I drifted into a nice fantasy, thinking of children, knowing that many women in their forties were having babies.

He asked, "Don't you feel tied down with a dog?"

Hmm. A yellow warning light flashed, but I pushed it from my mind.

After a while, released from her leash to roam freely, Amie darted ahead to sniff a Springer Spaniel. She rushed towards the stream and rolled in its muddy bank, blissfully unaware that she would later shiver, tail between legs when I'd put her in the shower.

Rick looked pensive. Squinting in the late afternoon sunlight, he asked, "Do you have perspective?"

"About what?" I countered. He raised his eyebrows and smiled. I sensed he was on to me and knew I was getting carried away with thoughts of a future.

Later, we went for dinner at a cozy French restaurant. As we flirted across the small table, eating salmon in a buttery lemon-garlic sauce, my doubts from our afternoon vanished. Afterward, when he was leaving, we hugged for a long time inside my front door.

On our second date a week later, Rick brought me a jar opener and a round piece of thin, white rubber shaped like—a daisy. We had dinner again at the same restaurant and talked about our families. His parents divorced, and his father remarried. "My father's wife and I get along famously," he said.

Oh, sure, I thought skeptically but said nothing. Ethel was technically my stepmother, but we rarely saw each other. When I wanted to talk to my father and she answered the phone, she'd usually call, "Oscar!" and hand it to him.

Rick had been married ten years earlier for six months. He said she was nice, but her clothes took up too much closet space. Another flashing yellow light, but I blocked it out. It was ten years ago, anyway.

Our next two dates were singles hiking club outings, Rick's idea both times. During the second one, while Rick walked ahead, Roberta asked me, "How come if you and Rick are seeing each other, he's taking you to singles events?" I mumbled how we both liked being with the group and noticed a tight feeling in my gut. During a rest stop, Rick came over, cheerfully suggesting dinner with the group. No, I said, picturing a long table filled with women he would charm and men I'd ignore because I wanted to be alone with him.

Later, we talked on the couch at my place about his planned trip to Israel in a few weeks. I missed him already. "What would you like to do next time we get together?" I asked casually.

"I'll check the club's schedule. Maybe there's something else coming up."

"I'd like to see you alone, get to know you better. That can't happen if we're with the group every time." *Whew*, I thought. *I'd said it!*

His face glowed as he moved to embrace me. "That makes me feel so good." Wow, he wasn't running away!

Not at the moment, but later, as we hugged and said good night, he said he resented my saying I didn't want to keep going to singles events with him.

Still held in his arms, I asked, "When will I see you again?"

His hold loosened. "I don't know." I waited, and in a few seconds, he again held me and murmured, "It feels so good to be close to you."

He loves me!

"Mm, I'd like to hear from you during the week. Will you call?" I wanted to play this out to the limit.

Silence. He let go and moved back enough for me to feel a chasm between us. I felt him cringe.

He loves me, not.

"How about Wednesday?" My mental calculator said it meant he loved me if he would agree to call on Wednesday. "Call me Wednesday, okay?"

He flinched, eyes cold now, blinking.

He loves me, not.

"Don't pressure me. I don't like pressure."

I waited until he moved in again to hold me, and we were again floating into bliss.

"It seems like a small thing to want to know when I'll see or hear from you."

Rick tensed as he backed away again.

Our back-and-forth dance continued while, inside, I continued to play the daisy game. Each time I eased up because *he loves me not* flashed through my mind, he relaxed and embraced me. Finally, at two a.m., we were exhausted and called it a night.

I was miserable for a couple of days, replaying our last conversation repeatedly. I hoped Rick would call, but my stomach's emptiness told me he wouldn't. Finally, I wrote him a letter. I might have spent months or longer hoping to win him over when I confused lust with love in the old days. I might have just called to say hi or invited him to dinner. When at my wits end, I might have sent him a letter that poured out my heart. Finally, I would give up and mourn for a long time before I could look at another man, which happened after Len and others.

I'd been in therapy with Dr. Posner long enough to know I was again going for an emotionally distant guy who provided the familiar and strangely comforting possibility that he'd abandon me. Men like Rick probably rekindled buried feelings about losing my father after the divorce.

I decided not to send the letter to Rick. Willing myself to calmness by breathing slowly and deeply, I phoned him and said, "I've been thinking about you."

"That's nice," he said, sounding friendly. "How are you?"

In the past, I would have suggested he come over for dinner. He would be delighted to come, and we two commitment-phobes would have been in business again.

But now, I said, "I was upset after our last conversation, but I feel much better about us now."

"Good," Rick said, apparently ready to continue the "come-close, make-distance" game. "I'm glad to hear that."

"I've noticed a pattern with us. It seems you back off each time you can tell I'm feeling closer to you."

He was silent. "Some people respond to intimacy that way," I continued. "That's fine if that's where you are, but it doesn't work for me."

After a pause, he asked, in a quiet voice, "We can still be friends, can't we?"

"Of course," I said, understanding he wanted to avoid awkwardness if our paths crossed, and I shouldn't badmouth him.

"Goodbye then," he said softly, sounding disappointed.

After we hung up, I stared at the phone, barely believing what happened. I wasn't sure which of us was more in shock. I felt high. Nothing unfinished, nothing to mourn.

By the next day, I was ready to plan a camping trip to Russian Gulch. "What do you think, Amie?" I asked, hugging her. "Just you and me." I felt like I could do anything.

38 – Secrets and Stigma

1987. Berkeley, California

"I just bought a tent and a sleeping bag," I told Dr. Posner, jubilant.

He looked concerned.

Was he thinking, Is she manic? Spending sprees can be a sign of mania.

"What inspired you to buy them?" Caution showed on the lines of his forehead.

"Are you worried that I'm becoming manic?" I sometimes wondered if I should be concerned, when I was simply high on life.

Dr. Posner looked noncommittal except for the deepened lines on his forehead.

Am I manic now? I thought. *No, that's silly. I've been dreaming about a camping trip with Amie.*

"I'm okay, really," I said. "I've wanted to camp at Russian Gulch State Park for a long time. Just Amie and me. I'll feel less vulnerable in a tent. The sleeping bag is easier to pack than my old one; it stuffs into a matching bag."

Dr. Posner's face relaxed. "So these were not impulsive purchases," he said. He sat back in his chair, waiting.

"I've never camped alone, but why should I wait for a group to make the trip or someone to go with me?" I yearned to be alone now, not looking for a new man and either failing at finding one or succeeding but ending up disappointed. "This campground is in a rustic, woodsy area in Mendocino. It has a hiking trail that leads to a waterfall."

"So you're preparing."

"Yes," I smiled, feeling validated.

"I don't anticipate a problem," Dr. Posner said gravely, "but it's time to test your lithium level."

That was fine with me. Testing every few months was crucial to tell whether someone's lithium level was adequate to prevent psychosis, but not so high as to increase the risk of harmful side effects, such as kidney damage.

My lithium level stayed about the same, well below the published therapeutic level, and effective with no evident side effects. Too grateful for my sanity to think about the possible future consequences of taking lithium, I expected to take it forever.

No matter how sanely I behaved, anyone who knew my psychiatric history might have evaluated me on a self-devised looniness scale for the rest of my life. I expected this from Dr. Posner. As my therapist, he was supposed to notice signs of mania and order blood tests.

So why did I feel a twinge of resentment this day?

Because I didn't want people to define me as crazy for buying a tent and sleeping bag, I didn't tell anyone my secret. I wanted acceptance for who I was, life experiences included. Yet, I didn't wish for reactions to my diagnosis—like "Is she all right?"—or glances toward me for knitting at a staff meeting. Or sexual harassment from a supervisor who thought he could get away with grabbing a vulnerable woman's breasts. Or ridicule with a song about "l-i-t-h-i-u-m" from a colleague who was way less psychologically healthy than I was.

Sometimes I felt guilty about holding back a vital part of my background, especially when someone shared very private information about themselves with me.

"What do other people who see you and who have a diagnosis like mine, manic-depression, do?" I asked Dr. Posner. "Do they tell people or keep it a secret?"

His head bobbed almost imperceptibly. "Sometimes people tell, and it works out fine. Other times, they are sorry they did."

Better to be safe. "What if I'd told the board and staff members about my diagnosis and lithium? I don't know whether my firing happened for going crazy at work or because they believed I'd fired Lorna."

I might have deserved being fired for a different reason: I lacked what it took to be a successful executive director. I came into a job lacking the experience or personal traits to do it well. I wasn't good at schmoozing with board and staff members or strategizing to get everyone willing to move in an agreed-on direction. But I doubt I was asked to resign for any of those reasons. Not after the board rewarded me with a hefty raise last year.

"Maybe they didn't know I was certifiably crazy." Unlike my former colleagues, these staff members were less well-trained and inexperienced with psychiatric patients. "But still ..."

Dr. Posner's face was blank.

"Am I in denial to believe that might even be possible? That no one knew I was psychotic, that they thought I was sick with a cold while in the hospital? I wonder if telling them about my condition would have made any difference."

"There is no way to know, of course, but whether you told them or not, there would have been a risk." He didn't say whether he believed my colleagues knew I was psychotic.

"Do you think anyone who doesn't know I have a psychiatric problem would guess I do now?"

"They would be surprised."

I thought about how I probably appeared to others: competent, attractive, well-dressed, and friendly—the owner of a lovely condominium with a pool and tennis courts, a nice car, and a small business.

The novelty of earning a living as an entrepreneur was still fresh. Suppliers of advertising specialties at trade shows loaded me with samples. I enjoyed my relationships with them and liked the challenge of developing ideas for promotional gifts for clients to give to their customers, employees, and others.

Dr. Posner mirrored my pleasure in my small triumphs in gaining corporate accounts, developing marketing solutions for my clients, and networking.

39 – Matchmaking

1987. Corte Madera, California

I'd heard Chabad rabbis liked to do matchmaking. I felt ready to meet someone vetted by an expert. So I went to a fundraising art auction for Chabad of Marin to meet Rabbi Chaim Rothstein and ask for his help.

Chabad, I learned, is a Hasidic branch of Orthodox Judaism. Before meeting Rabbi Rothstein, all I knew about Hasidic Jews was that they seemed quite different from the rest of us. I'd seen some in Brooklyn when I was fourteen. On our way home from shopping, my mother and I sat near the back of a bus. Odd-looking people boarded along the way: women wearing scarves that hid their hair and clothes covering them almost entirely, long-sleeved blouses, and long skirts. The men had beards and wore black hats with brims, black suits, and white shirts. The boys had forelocks in front of their ears, like their fathers, but they wore yarmulkes.

I looked at my mother questioningly. She whispered, "They're Hasidic Jews. They're clannish; they stick to themselves." Looking again, I sensed an otherworldly manner in them. The children, too, looked somber.

Rabbi Rothstein was Hasidic but not clannish. Twenty-eight and stocky, he had dark-red hair, a thick beard, and a friendly manner. Chabad Lubavitchers are typically outgoing. They reach out to Jewish people, particularly nonobservant ones. They want to help them live more Torah-observant lives.

"I hear that you like to fix people up," I told the Rabbi at the art show after introducing myself. "I want to get married." *There, I'd said it.*

The rabbi remained composed, like he was hearing nothing new. "How old are you?"

"Forty-two." *Uh-oh. He may think I'm too old to have children and not want to bother.*

Eileen said she read that a single woman over forty had as much chance of marrying as being run over by a truck.

"Do you want children?"

"Yes." I believed this was still possible. My mother's medicine cabinet had tampons when she was past fifty, so I was optimistic about conceiving.

"I want to invite you to Shabbos dinner this Friday. We'll eat, then we'll talk."

When I arrived that evening, he greeted me cheerily. "Come in, come in!" He wore a black frock coat, crisp, white dress shirt, and black fedora. "You're in time for candle lighting."

Silver candlesticks gleamed on the dining table, where several guests were seated. Rabbi Rothstein's wife, Chani, lit the candles, closed her eyes, covered them with her hands, and recited a blessing to welcome the Sabbath. She stood still, her lips moving in silent prayer. The stiff fabric of her high-necked, blue satin dress, which reflected the chandelier's light, had puffy sleeves that accented her slim figure and delicate bone structure. Opening her eyes, Chani smiled radiantly and wished us "Good Shabbos!"

"Good Shabbos, Good Shabbos!" Rabbi Rothstein beamed. "I hope you're ready to sing from the sheets before you. Don't be shy." The first song welcomed the Sabbath angels. Rabbi Rothstein kept the beat, tapping, then pounding on the table with his hands. We sang "Puff the Kosher Dragon," "Pop-eye the Sailor Mensch," and "Ain't Gonna Work on Saturday."

Some of us giggled at these humorous children's songs, which affirm the value of living Jewishly: Puff keeps kosher, and if a dragon can, so can we; Pop-eye bentches, which means he says the required prayer after a meal. The last song is about a hulky construction guy who refuses to work on the Sabbath even for double or triple pay because he "ain't gonna work on Saturday."

When the rabbi's plump baby boy wasn't in his father's lap, he bounced in his high chair and clapped while we sang. Feeling like part of a large, joyful family, I almost forgot why I'd come.

Rabbi Rothstein stood to say the Kiddish prayer over a cup of wine, and I rose with the others. He said the blessing over the challah I remembered saying with other children at overnight summer camps. I talked with other guests over a festive meal with gefilte fish, chicken soup, roast chicken, potato kugel, and vegetables.

Rivka, her husband, Joseph, and two other Marin couples had been seeking a more meaningful Jewish life. They helped arrange for Rabbi Rothstein to move here from Brooklyn to lead a fledgling Marin congregation.

Rivka was petite and pregnant. Joseph, an insurance broker, was over six feet tall. They were friendly, and I felt at home with them. Like me, they were from New York, where they met at City College.

Another couple at the table had a daughter attending Chani's preschool. "We grew up in assimilated families," the husband said, "but we want more for our child. Chani makes learning about the holidays, the Torah, and the mitzvot fun. Our daughter loves it."

The large bookcase behind my seat was filled with Jewish books. Some were in sets of many volumes with leather covers embossed in gold. A framed wedding photograph of Rabbi and Chani Rothstein sat on one shelf.

Chani was from Australia. She and Rabbi Rothstein were introduced when she attended a seminary in the Crown Heights Brooklyn neighborhood, where he was learning at a yeshiva. "I wasn't in a hurry to marry," she said, "but Chaim was, and I agreed to meet him. He was twenty-six, and I was twenty-four."

"He already knew he wanted to come here," Chani continued. "These Marin families had been learning from an Orthodox rabbi in San Francisco. They wanted a Chabad rabbi closer to their homes for the High Holidays, and that rabbi helped them make arrangements."

"So that's how I came here over two years ago," Rabbi Rothstein said. "It was a good match for the community and me. They wanted me here full-time, but a Chabad rabbi must be married before leading a congregation. I had my first date with Chani, then another, and we got engaged. Six weeks later, we were married."

Chani picked up on my surprised expression, "That's not unusual. Hasidishe people don't date for recreation like people do in the popular culture. When we're ready to marry, someone who knows us and our families arranges for an introduction. If it feels right after one date, you have another, and by the second or third . . . you know." Her husband nodded, and they exchanged smiles.

Hasidic dating! This blew my mind. It was so different from how my friends and I dated. And they looked happy together; her calmness seemed to complement his exuberance.

Over cake, Rabbi Rothstein's voice became soft, almost hypnotic, as he told a story about Reb Zusha of Anipoli, a learned Hasid who lived over two centuries ago. The rabbi explained, "After a person dies and ascends to the heavens for judgment, he must defend his past actions and behavior."

I listened without knowing what to think. I wasn't used to musing about G-d or an afterlife.

Rabbi Rothstein said that Reb Zusha was quaking with fright on his deathbed. He wasn't afraid of being asked why he wasn't great, like Moses. He feared being asked, "Why weren't you Zusha?" Rabbi Rothstein sipped some water and continued, "We are given special abilities and will be required to explain why we have not fully used our G-d-given talents. The only person each of us will be compared to is ourself. Did we use our talents to the fullest? Were we as great as we could have been?"

While taking in his words, unlike anything I'd learned in my scant religious training, I'd drifted into an enjoyable trance. I came out of it when Joseph handed out small booklets that included the prayer said after a meal. Like Pop-eye, we opened them and "bentched."

Rabbi Rothstein led me to a quiet corner of his living room. He sat on the couch, and I took a chair next to him. As he looked into my eyes, I felt like the only person in his world.

"Nu," he said, a Yiddish expression meaning something like, "So what gives?" I shrugged my shoulders and looked down. "You want to get married?"

"Yes."

"So?"

"I've had a lot of boyfriends. The ones I want don't want to commit. The ones that want to get serious, I eventually run away from them."

"The problem is that the men you get involved with are interested in your body, not your soul."

Chills coursed through me. Words that usually would have sounded like a cliché reached deep within me, to my essence or *soul*.

How had this happened? Was it Rabbi Rothstein's undivided attention? His penetrating get-to-the-heart-of-things manner? Nothing new was on the surface of his words, but these were about my soul.

Then I remembered what I'd come for, to ask him to help me get married.

"Will you introduce me to someone?"

"First, you must become a proper Jewish woman."

What does he mean? Aren't I proper enough? I know he doesn't mean to insult me, but still. Maybe he means I can use a few finishing touches. Something like the gold embossment on his leather-bound books. Or the icing on tonight's cake.

"There's a two-week program at Bais Channa, a Lubavitcher school in Minnesota, where you can learn the basics; it's a good place to start. Their next session begins in a few weeks."

Going to Bais Channa sounded extreme. I didn't want to get brainwashed, just married. And I didn't want to take an expensive, time-consuming trip when, in my mind, I already was a proper Jewish woman.

"I don't know," I said as we rose to help clear the table. "I might look into it."

"Come back again for Shabbos dinner," he said. "You're always welcome."

40 – A Singles Event

1987. San Francisco, California

Eileen drove us to a singles event at Temple Emanuel, the large, domed San Francisco synagogue. In a long-sleeved, bright-red dress that flared below my knees, I was dressed for success in attracting men.

Eileen said as we approached the Golden Gate Bridge, "You still haven't told me about last Friday at the rabbi's home. Will he fix you up?"

"Not exactly. Rabbi Rothstein said first I'd have to go to this place in Minnesota for a week or two to learn how to be a proper Jewish woman. I'm not ready for that, and why would I need it?"

"Oh, well, at least you tried, but that does seem a bit rigid of him—"

"Not really; he has a standard and allowed me to meet it by going there. I'm the one saying no. Maybe I'm the rigid one, but it feels too extreme."

"I couldn't imagine doing *that*," she said. "I wouldn't fit in with those people. Their way of being Jewish is different from the mainstream, you know."

"It's different, all right. But Rabbi Rothstein and his wife seem so happy."

"I mean different sexually."

I snapped to attention.

"They do it through a hole in a sheet."

My mouth dropped open. "Where did you hear that?"

"Oh, word gets around."

"Are you sure you heard right?"

"You don't forget when you hear something like that."

She was right about not forgetting. It would stick in my mind until I found out the truth.

Momentarily distracted by maneuvering in the heavy traffic, Eileen said nothing else for a minute. I continued to fill her in on my meeting with Rabbi Rothstein. I had phoned to thank him for having me over. In his husky voice, he'd asked cheerily, "So what about Minnesota?" I hesitated, until he gave me the name and number of someone in San Francisco who'd been there.

"It doesn't hurt to inquire," he had said. "One phone call. What do you have to lose?"

Trying to keep an open mind, I did call her. Even though the other "girls" were much younger, she liked the Minnesota program. After coming home, she koshered her kitchen.

"And?" Eileen prompted.

"I thought that was nice for her, but I wasn't ready. I'm not saying *never*, just not now—too many negatives: the cost, the cold weather, and the timing. So now I'm back to my usual ways of meeting a man. I wonder how many single ones are left in the world I haven't already met."

"Lots are in the world, but maybe not many in the San Francisco Bay area." She grinned mischievously. I was glad Eileen's sense of humor was back. When we talked the night before, she moped about a guy who dumped her. I was secretly glad. He was a slob.

"Someone new could show up, maybe someone who just moved here," Eileen said, tongue in cheek. "Or someone who just got divorced, or—"

"You're trying to cheer me up," I accused, smiling. "You don't have to. I'm okay. There are probably at least ten men in a hundred-mile radius I haven't met." She laughed. "Anyway, now that I'm dying my hair, one of them might notice me."

I wanted to age gracefully. But I gave up on letting my gray hairs show after having felt invisible to men after I used to attract them effortlessly.

"Yeah, right!" she smiled.

I was worried about Eileen. I had to twist her arm to get her to come to this singles event. She insisted on driving so she could leave if she wanted to. "Are you up for this?" I asked.

The man who left her life had greasy hair and skin, and his shirt slopped out of his dirty jeans. Eileen told me he had body odor and tracked mud from his boots onto her carpet. He lashed out at her for being critical when she complained to him.

I wished Eileen would realize her worth and know she deserved better.

"What do I have to lose?" she said. "We'll get dinner and have each other to talk to if we don't meet anyone. I don't expect to find someone until I lose weight."

Eileen's shoulder-length, honey-blond hair glistened, framing her rosy complexion and effervescent smile. She was a bit overweight but still gorgeous. I remembered hearing my mother say some men prefer fat women; "they like to get lost in the folds." She wasn't saying I should get fat. She was probably rambling out loud, trying to figure out why her marriage hadn't lasted and others had.

"Give some nice guy a chance. You're still a knockout. And you're smart and funny. Think positive." She nodded dismissively, but her lips hinted at a smile.

I wasn't expecting to meet anyone, just hoping to enjoy the evening. Thinking this way prevented me from sending out desperate vibes that repelled good men and attracted the wrong kind.

At Temple Emanuel's social hall, two candlesticks sat on large round tables covered with white cloths. When the event coordinator asked for a volunteer at each table to light the candles,

I rose. Picturing Chani Rothstein, I closed my eyes while saying the blessing.

After the buffet dinner, we moved to chairs lined up to face a big screen. We watched a black-and-white movie about the heydays of the Borscht Belt in the Catskills mountains in upstate New York. These all-inclusive resorts were popular vacation spots for New York City Jews from the 1920s through the 1960s. Most were gone by the 1970s.

Two of the most impressive Borscht Belt resorts were Grossinger's and the Concord hotels. I'd stayed at the Concord a few years before for a national conference for Jewish Family Service agencies' executive directors and board members. During my first lunch in the dining room, I was shocked to watch an attractive woman at my table point to four or five gourmet desserts she selected from a waiter's tray. She seemed to model entitlement until I learned this was normal behavior at these places.

Some singles gatherings seemed like "meat-markets," but this one at Temple Emanuel felt like a relaxed gathering of down-to-earth, friendly people. A buffet dessert followed the movie about the Borscht Belt. People chatted while standing and eating cookies and cake.

Eileen said some people she'd talked with wanted to go to a nearby bar. "Please say you'll come," she urged. "I met a nice guy, and he's going, and this woman I met is also going, and also a guy she met."

A smoky bar wasn't my idea of fun, but she was my ride home. "Okay," I said, "but I don't want to be a fifth wheel."

"You can invite some people to come along. We'll go in five minutes."

My path toward the desserts crossed that of a slim, dark-haired man with a mustache. He looked under thirty, but I wasn't thinking about age when I smiled at him; I was just being friendly.

"Hi," I said. His eyes lit up. I sensed kindness in them and calmness in his appearance. He was wearing a navy suit. "I'm Marcia."

"Hi, I'm David."

What a sweet smile, I thought. "A group of us are going out somewhere for a drink. Maybe you'd like to join us?" I said.

"Sure. Where?"

I told him, adding breezily, "If you want to invite anyone else, feel free." The more, the merrier.

"See you there, then," I said, thinking about who else to ask. I approached the next man whose path crossed mine. His name was Howard, and he also looked too young for me. I told him about the bar. He seemed pleased and said he'd come.

When Eileen and I arrived at the bar, we joined the others around a low table. Eileen sat near the man she liked, a podiatrist. On the other side of her, David and Howard talked. Next to them conversed a good-looking real estate broker and the woman Eileen befriended at the temple's event. I sat between the two potential new couples.

When I tried to join the conversation with Eileen's new friend and the man she liked, the former shot daggers at me with her eyes. Turning back to him, she placed her hand on his thigh.

I wanted to give Eileen time with the man she was interested in, but I felt isolated. I leaned past the podiatrist and asked her, "When can we leave?"

"Just a little longer, okay?"

"Okay, but I have no one to talk to."

"Why don't you change seats with me? Then you can talk to these two guys," she said, glancing toward David and Howard.

We did that, and I talked with the two sweet, young men, both accountants.

"I can use some accounting help," I said lightly. "I have this business and want to set up my books to make sense." I babbled on for a while about my advertising specialties business, and they expressed interest and asked questions. "I'm learning as I go," I said. "I don't know whether it will succeed, but it's exciting for now, and I'm putting in a lot more time than when I had a boss. It's different when it's your own thing."

They seemed so young and sincere. *It would have been nice to have a brother*, I thought. I felt relaxed as we talked about our work, the awkwardness of the singles scene, and whatever else came up. I sensed we were passing the time, aware that our age difference ruled out anything more.

The dagger lady and the realtor had left arm in arm. I caught Eileen's eye. "It's getting late," I mouthed.

"Okay."

As we walked toward her car, she said, "He took my phone number."

"Good," I said, yawning. "Then it was worth it."

41 – Hasidic Sex

1987. San Rafael, California

A t Rabbi Rothstein and Chani's home the following Friday night, I sat with Chani in the kitchen after we cleared the dishes from the dining room table. I wanted to ask her if what Eileen heard about the Orthodox way of having sex was true, but I feared offending her.

"Maybe you have some questions," Chani said in her bright Australian accent. "Most people do."

"Well . . . I—"

"The last time we talked, you seemed surprised that Hasidic people marry so quickly."

A surge of warmth filled my cheeks. "This is sort of awkward, but I heard . . . it's kind of personal, I—"

"Do you mean about the hole in the sheet?" she laughed, looking at me.

"So it's not true." What a relief because, if it were, I'd wonder if I'd stumbled into a cult and plan my escape.

"The Torah says we're supposed to enjoy sex; it's not just for procreation. A Jewish husband must satisfy his wife and treat her with respect and kindness."

This sounded better and better.

"I don't know who thought up that nonsense about cutting a hole in a sheet, but it's nothing like that. We're not intimate before marriage, but that makes it so special when it happens." Chani said spouses who observe Jewish laws, as defined in the Torah, refrain from physical intimacy during the wife's menstrual period and for seven more days. They don't even touch.

"It's a good thing, all in all," she said. "When you get back together each month, after going to the *mikveh*, a ritual bath, the wife feels like a new bride again, and her husband appreciates her more for the waiting."

"So it's like abstinence making the heart grow fonder?" I grinned.

"Something like that," Chani said, smiling. "When you don't have sex to fall back on as a way to connect, you learn to communicate in other ways, so you become friends when you can't be lovers. Also, you get back your identity as a separate person."

Interesting, I thought, *if a bit of a culture shock.*

"This is part of the *mitzvah* of family purity or *Taharat Ha-Mishpakha*," Chani said. It's one of Jewish women's three primary mitzvot. The others are Shabbos (Sabbath) observance—including candle lighting—and keeping a kosher home."

Driving home, I thought about Shabbos being a special mitzvah for women. I remembered giving a talk at a Reform synagogue in Fremont for Jewish Family Service. I talked about the need many of us have to learn ways to slow down in our busy, stressful lives. I mentioned meditation as one example, among other ways to relax. The rabbi who'd invited me to lecture added, "The Sabbath is an important way to relax and renew ourselves." I felt embarrassed for not having mentioned that. But as Andrew had noticed, I knew little about Jewish religious practices back then.

As I lay in bed that night, I was happy and sad—glad to have been at Rabbi Rothstein and Chani's home, yet keenly aware of my aloneness now.

Sleep eluded me. Scenes flashed in my mind: singing at the dining room table. Rivka whispering in her husband's ear, and he smiling. Rabbi Rothstein and Chani laughing. Chani and I talking in the kitchen.

After some tossing and turning, I knew what to do: an experiment. Tomorrow, Saturday, I would observe the Sabbath. No driving, no answering the phone, no turning the lights on or off, no cooking.

Satisfied, I drifted off to sleep.

42 – The Sabbath Experiment

No French toast or scrambled eggs for me that morning. Cold cereal with milk, topped with banana, was good enough. No driving on the Sabbath either, so errands would wait. What would I do instead? I was at loose ends and couldn't even use the phone. Sabbath observance seemed to be a list of *don'ts*. Don't cook, write, play music, watch television, or turn lights on or off. I knew what *not* to do, but what *could* I do?

I sat on my couch scanning the pages of San Francisco's *Jewish Bulletin*. Beneath the announcements of engagements, marriages, and fiftieth wedding anniversaries, a small headline announced: "National Jewish Singles Cruise." The print below stated that it would be to the Caribbean in March, a week-long, yearly event resulting in many marriages. Space was limited, so the deposit should be sent soon.

I'd been only half-joking when I told Eileen I'd met all the available local men. This cruise could be a fun vacation and a way to meet new ones.

I'd been husband-hunting for so long that it felt like part of my identity, a natural thing to do. I'd complained to Dr. Posner about how much effort it took to keep my eyes open for ways to meet a new man. "Why must I go through all this? Why can't someone find me a husband?"

"In an ideal world …" he'd said evenly, leaving me to complete the thought.

These words were almost as familiar to me as his homey office with piles of journals on a small table, his psychoanalyst-style couch, unused in my therapy, and the softness of his eyes. I'd been spilling out my insides every week for two years. *An ideal world* meant the world was not perfect; I should accept reality instead of expecting pipe dreams to come true.

I set the *Bulletin* on the table, thinking that the perfect husband would soon arrive at my door in an ideal world, and I wouldn't have to go national to find a husband. *Oh, well.*

I smiled. After discussing a disappointment with Dr. Posner once, I'd said, "Oh, well."

"Yes," he said, nodding, "Oh, well," implying that I'd given a healthy response to a frustrating experience. I'd felt complimented for making progress.

Later that afternoon, I walked a mile to Betty's house. Thinking I'd buy a newspaper from a rack on the way back, I put a quarter in my knapsack. I felt virtuous about not driving, not yet having learned that observing the Sabbath includes not buying and not carrying things outside. Betty looked happy to see me and stared at my knapsack.

"I walked over. I'm observing the Sabbath today, as the Orthodox do."

"Oh," she said, with a faint, amused smile, indulging her quirky friend. "Shelly will be here any minute. We're driving to the new Mexican restaurant for an early dinner. Do you want to come?"

"I can't. I'm observing the Sabbath. Thanks anyway."

Shelly arrived. "Hi, Marcia. Are you coming with us?"

"She can't; she's Orthodox," Betty said, implying this was a good joke. I was getting a kick out of behaving so uncharacteristically. We three belonged to the local Reform synagogue.

I was pleased with what I was doing and felt like my own person. Cars whizzed by as I walked back home along Sir Francis Drake Boulevard. I felt content spending the day on my schedule and at my own pace. I bought a newspaper from the rack and put it in my knapsack. *I like the Sabbath*, I thought while walking uphill to my condo.

Inside, it was dark. Amie excitedly greeted me at the door, and we took a short walk. Home again, I ignored the ringing phone, feeling free. I hardly minded the dark, unavoidable because the Sabbath had begun when I decided to do the experiment. If I did this again, I'd turn on a light or two before the Sabbath started.

What to do in the dark? I plopped onto the waterbed for a nap; Amie joined me. When I woke up, I looked at the sky from my patio. It twinkled with stars. Okay! I said; it's over. Amie licked my leg just above my sock. I rubbed the fur on the back of her neck. She turned her face up toward mine and looked at me adoringly. I felt like her whole world.

I turned on some lights and wrote a check at my desk five months before the trip to reserve my National Jewish Singles Cruise spot. *No reason to wait.*

43 – David

1987. Greenbrae, California

David, the too-young-for-me accountant, phoned to ask me out to a play. He said he'd bring some bookkeeping sheets and show me how to use them for my business. We saw *Brigadoon*. Its romance and surrealistic, misty stage effects transported me to another world. I loved it.

Afterward, I showed David my home office, where promotional gift samples—mugs, pen sets, clocks, watches, atlases, key tags, T-shirts, caps, appointment books, and catalogs—filled shelves. I could show my clients these things to help them choose suitable gifts to buy for their organization's employees, customers, or prospective clients. I arranged for my factories to put the company's logo and customized message on the ordered items.

"Wow, it's busy here," David said.

Uh-oh! The framed diplomas on a wall showed my college and grad school graduation years—my age. I stepped in front of the certificates to block his view and said, "How about some tea and dessert?" and edged us toward the living room. "Then we can have the bookkeeping lesson."

Safely seated at the dining table, I said, "I'm enjoying my business, the novelty of doing something different, and new challenges."

"I can see it's exciting for you. I'm doing something different too. I quit a high-pressure job as a controller at a large medical clinic a year ago. I was there for nine years and worked sixty hours a week during the last two. Finally, I'd had enough and quit. I felt like I'd gotten my life back."

"Me too," I said. "I felt that way after leaving my executive director job; it was so consuming." Like me, David must have been exhausted.

He nodded. "So after that, I wanted to take it easy. I needed a break. I'm working a couple of days a week for a contractor who buys and fixes apartment buildings to rent out or sell. He and his wife live on a ranch in Los Gatos with horses; that's where I work. I like having free time to relax, go to the gym, hike, and catch up with friends."

David removed a few bookkeeping sheets from his briefcase. He showed me how to list accounts, label the columns, and record billing and payment details.

"Thank you so much," I said. "You've made it much easier to keep track of the money."

When he said goodbye, he bent down to give me the most gentle kiss on the cheek. His sweetness moved me. I felt light and warm. I liked his looks too: his chiseled face, olive complexion, dark brown hair, and sexy eyes.

After David left, I covered the graduation dates on my diplomas with tiny yellow Post-it notes.

David and I started getting together weekly; as friends, I thought, because of our age difference. I liked his company, sincerity, and sense of humor. I wasn't dating anyone else, and he didn't seem to mind driving over an hour to see me. I liked talking to him when he phoned before bedtime on weeknights. His calm voice and interest in my daily life soothed me and helped me drift off to sleep after saying goodnight.

One sunny Sunday afternoon on our third time out, David and I took Amie to Piper Park in Corte Madera, next to the town's police station. We watched her explore the expansive grassy field from our spot on a blanket he'd brought from his car.

We talked about EST (an acronym for Erhard Seminars Training), a wildly popular human potential program. The events were held in the 1970s and early '80s in hotel ballrooms in the United States and beyond. David said he'd signed up for the training while having a rough time. I couldn't picture him in a massive room with about two hundred enthusiastic workshop participants. David seemed more low-key than those I'd known who'd raved about their EST experience.

What rough time was he referring to? I wondered but didn't want to pry.

"So, how was EST?"

"It was good. I learned I can be a real jerk," David smiled.

I liked that he could say that. He had a good sense of humor and could let down his guard.

"I never took the EST training, but my mother did."

His eyes widened. "Your mother went to EST?"

"I know that sounds strange; she was about seventy then. She refused to obey their rules about not eating, drinking, or going to the bathroom for long periods. My mother told them, 'I have an ulcer; an operation removed two-thirds of my stomach. I need to eat often.' She sat in the back row and didn't wait to use the restroom. She snacked on foods in her knapsack—cottage cheese, sliced carrots, celery, or fruit."

David laughed. "She must have given them a run for their money."

My mother told me the training gave her the courage to confront my father. She'd worked herself up about my father's lack of attention to Gloria's young children. Mom phoned him, saying, "I need to talk to you about something important." She asked him to meet her in front of the EST building in Manhattan, a large, multi-storied brick structure. There, she told my father, "Your grandchildren need you. You should visit them more often. Phone them too; keep in touch."

I'd been so fascinated by my mother's story that I barely noticed how I felt put in the middle by her again when she confided in me about that conversation she'd had with my father.

"It might have done my mother some good if she'd gone to EST," David said wistfully. "Maybe she'd still be alive if she had." His mother died ten years ago. His parents had a good marriage.

David took a deep breath. "She must have been panic-stricken when the doctor said she had colon cancer. She was in her fifties and had recently lost several of her closest friends to cancer. Even though the doctor told her that with an operation and treatment, her chances of surviving were eighty percent, she didn't want to go through what her friends did—the surgeries, the chemotherapy ..."

I closed my eyes, dreading what he'd say next.

"She did it in our garage, attached one end of the hose to the exhaust pipe, and put the other inside the car to fill it with carbon monoxide. My youngest brother came home and found her there."

"How awful." So that must be the rough time David had gone through. Now, his lips trembled. His pain felt fresh. Part of me wanted to reach out and hold him, but he looked like he was trying to accept something he couldn't change.

I felt closer to David. How devastating for him and the family. I felt like I could talk to him about anything.

Well, not *anything*. Not my age, my psychotic episodes, or lithium. It was too risky to tell anyone before a commitment happened.

It felt natural to ask David casually whether he hoped to marry eventually. He said yes, and he wanted to be a parent. *That's nice*, I thought; *we're talking abstractly.*

"You're young; you have plenty of time."

"I'm not that young," he said.

Right, you're under thirty; I'm forty-three.

"Don't think you're fooling me with those Post-it notes on your diplomas. I saw them before you covered the dates."

My cheeks heated up. "So you made a point to look," I said accusingly.

He shrugged and grinned.

I felt more admiration than resentment. I probably would have looked too.

"But you still wanted to go out with me again, even though I'm so much older—"

"You're not so much older—"

"Aren't you twenty-something?"

"I'm thirty-eight."

Hmm, that puts a different spin on things.

It was time to leave the park. I blew my whistle for Amie, and she came running. David and I folded the blanket. As we drove past the police station by the park's entrance, I realized this was the workplace of the two strapping young officers who had banged on my door three years ago. I could almost hear them yelling: "POLICE. OPEN UP." They'd driven me handcuffed to Marin General Hospital, where attendants strapped me to a table and injected me with Thorazine before moving me to the nearby acute psychiatric hospital in Ross.

No need to share such details with David or anyone else. I'll reveal them to the right person at the right time.

44 – The Skolye Rebbe

At one a.m., I stood with a small crowd upstairs at the Best Western Hotel in Corte Madera. Each of us awaited a private consultation with Rabbi Rabinowitz, the Skolye Rebbe, from Brooklyn, New York.

He was part of a Hasidic dynasty named after the town of Skole, or *Skolye* in Yiddish, in Eastern Galicia, which is currently in Ukraine, where the founder of this line of distinguished rebbes lived. A rebbe, I learned, is a righteous rabbi on a very high soul level. His purpose is to help others achieve their soul's purpose.

Earlier that evening, I heard the Skolye Rebbe lecture downstairs to an attentive audience of over a hundred people. He was heavyset and looked to be about thirty. Someone said he had six children. His black hat, thick, dark, untrimmed beard, and black suit accented his serious expression. His voice was barely audible, and he spoke with a thick Yiddish accent about concepts I was unfamiliar with.

Although I'd barely understood his words, I felt from the large turnout and the long list of people who'd signed up for a private consultation with him that I'd miss a rare opportunity if I didn't add my name.

So I waited outside with the others.

A couple of black-hatted, bearded Hasidim stood around. One of them called who was next on the list. The door to the room for consultations stayed slightly ajar when a woman was inside with Rabbi Rabinowitz. That seemed odd. People were here to discuss private matters. "Should we close the door?" I asked no one in particular.

"No," said one of the black hats quietly. "With certain exceptions, the laws of *yichud* do not permit a woman and man who are not married to each other to be alone with the door closed."

Okay. I let myself float into this seemingly alien culture. Being here at this hour was strange enough; nothing should have surprised me.

I sensed something beyond what I was gaining from therapy. The night was black as we stood on the landing under a small light. Mostly, we were quiet. Occasionally, a brief murmured exchange or the calling out of the list's next name broke the silence.

It was late, but I was wide awake, feeling something important in the air. Finally, I heard my name called. Nervous, I entered the room. The coordinator almost closed the door behind me, leaving an opening of an inch. The Skolye Rebbe was standing. As he sat, he gestured for me to take the empty chair facing his.

What would I say to this stranger? Could he relate to my issues? I might as well get it out.

As he continued to look straight ahead, I said, "I want to get married, but I'm afraid it won't work." My voice was shaking.

"How old are you?"

"Forty-three."

"Going on thirty-five," he said, his lips curling just enough to suggest a smile, or was it a sneer? He spoke softly but was easy to understand. His Yiddish accent seemed less pronounced; maybe I was getting used to it.

Was he making a joke? Did he think I was being ridiculous, that I was too old to marry? That I tried to pass myself off as younger? Or was he giving me a strange-sounding compliment because he's more adept at Yiddish than English? I felt too intimidated and vulnerable to press for his meaning.

"So, why shouldn't you get married?" he asked. "Do you have someone?"

I was blank for a second. Then, I almost whispered to myself, "David?" I was surprised to say his name and uncertain whether the Skolye Rebbe heard me.

David and I had had several dates by then, including one for Thanksgiving dinner with his father and other family members. When I went to New York for a few days, he took care of Amie. He drove me to the airport. On the way, David slipped a photograph of himself into my hand; I supposed so I would think of him and maybe show it to my relatives. When he picked me up on my return, Amie looked well cared for. She happily wagged her tail as she stood on the back seat of David's Integra, nose pressed against the window to greet me.

But marriage to David? After talking with Rabbi Rothstein, I'd stayed physically distant enough to maintain objectivity instead of letting hormones trick me into believing anyone was *the one*. I wasn't thinking about marriage to any particular person.

I pondered the Skolye Rebbe's question: *Why shouldn't I get married?*

"I think I want to get married, but I'm afraid it won't work and ..." Could I bring myself to say I'm manic-depressive, take lithium, and have been hospitalized? Could I trust this person, and tell him I feared marriage and motherhood would push me over the edge?

It was two a.m. As I faced the Skolye Rebbe, I believed he had extraordinary powers to help people. I sensed a lightness that set me at ease, and I expected he'd keep my secret. But would he think I was too damaged for marriage when he knew my truth?

"I'm frightened."

"It's okay; you can tell me anything. I remember everything. You can phone me in Brooklyn anytime if you have more questions."

I'd been holding my breath. I exhaled a rush of air. "If I tell you something about myself that I don't tell many people, will you keep it a secret?"

He nodded almost imperceptibly.

"I have a psychiatric diagnosis called manic-depression and take pills to keep myself stable, lithium." I was trembling all over. My eyes began to tear while my breath caught in my throat. "I just don't know if I can have a successful marriage," I gasped.

I was sobbing, ashamed, as though I'd confessed something awful about myself—a defect that would disqualify me as a wife to any good man. "Also, my parents divorced; my mother never got over it."

"Marriage will be good for you," he said.

Would the Skolye Rebbe think differently when I said what I've never said aloud before? "My mother's father abandoned her mother, my grandmother, when she was pregnant with my mother. She spent the rest of her life in an institution for mentally ill people. If I marry, I'm afraid I'll lose my husband and get locked up for life like her."

"You should definitely get married," he said.

My mouth dropped open. "Really?"

"It would be the best thing for you."

No one had ever said *that* to me. "I also wonder about being a mother. I think I can still get pregnant, but I'm scared I won't be able to handle it."

"You should do it. That, too, will be good for you."

I stared at him, incredulous. I wanted so much to believe him that I almost did.

Then he said, "It won't be perfect, but it will be ninety-seven percent. You can expect ninety-seven percent."

Ninety-seven percent. Why not one hundred percent? I thought Rabbi Rabinowitz was saying my defect would cause my marriage to be deficient, and I guessed he was right.

Still, ninety-seven percent was a pretty good prediction. This man saw all of me and said to go for everything I wanted. My fears dissolved, for the moment anyway.

Before I left, he reminded me that I could call him in Brooklyn anytime, and he'd remember everything. He gave me his telephone number.

Outside in the black mist, the air felt fresh against my skin. In a trance-like state, I took a few deep breaths, found my car, and drove home.

45 – Panicking

1988. Oakland, California

David came to see me every week for three months. Between dates, he phoned for leisurely talks close to my bedtime. He listened well and expressed interest in my advertising business. I told him about a new corporate account I'd landed and a visit from a manufacturer's representative who left samples, because samples sell.

I filled my office with imprinted jackets, calendars, clocks, pen sets, desk accessories, and other promotional items from various reps. If a picture is worth a thousand words, a sample's worth a million. Over a thousand factories produce imprinted business gifts and promotional items. "They need us to show and sell their products," I told David.

"They trust you to do the job."

David talked about the guys he worked for who lived close to the edge while buying, fixing, selling, and renting real estate. He worked out at a gym, played bridge, and hiked. Our chats nourished me.

I wasn't trying to turn our friendship into something big, just enjoying it without building sandcastles that could devastate me when they washed away. David was almost boyishly shy and not pushy physically, which I appreciated. He was kind and easy to be with. I still socialized at singles events and went out occasionally with someone else, keeping my options open.

Although I'd stopped playing the daisy game, I still found "warts." I complained to Dr. Posner about how David peppered his sentences with "ums and ahs." He sometimes said "or something" or "you know" twice in one sentence. He limped because, although he was a strong hiker, he had a rare neurological condition called Charcot-Marie-Tooth disease. He laughed at his own jokes and smiled too much.

"There are worse faults than smiling and wanting to be liked," Dr. Posner said.

I couldn't disagree. What was so bad about being with a man who wanted to please me?

"You are afraid of being abandoned, so you are trying to find an excuse to push him away before he leaves you."

Bingo.

I'd come smack up against my fear of abandonment on an early date with David. After dinner at Yet Wah in Larkspur Landing Saturday night, we went to A Clean, Well-Lighted Place for Books, my then-favorite bookstore. I gathered a few books and sat at a table in the back of the store, my usual reading spot.

I felt reassured when I looked up and saw David perusing books in an aisle. After a while, he said he'd go to a nearby market to get us drinks; then we could sit by the fountain outside with them.

Good idea, I thought, figuring he'd return in ten minutes.

Twenty minutes later, I wondered what was taking him so long. I stared at the page before me but couldn't focus. My chest tightened, and my breathing became shallow. *He's not coming back.*

I told Dr. Posner, "I was sure he was gone for good. Like when a wife says about a former husband, 'He said he was going out for a newspaper, and I never saw him again.'"

"Finally, David came with two bottles of lemonade."

I sensed an all-knowing expression on Dr. Posner's face, an I-told-you attitude. He was right; I thought I wanted marriage but felt destined to be abandoned. So I avoided that inevitable pain by harping on the faults of any prospective husband until one of us moved on. Yet even though I had been itemizing David's shortcomings, I panicked when I thought he'd left for good.

I almost heard my mother's words, "Is he still nice?" *Why expect any man to be more faithful than my father or her father had been? Sure, they're nice at first* . . .

"Do you think my getting sick on New Year's Eve was my way of trying to push David away?" I asked Dr. Posner in our next session. I'd gotten a stomach ache at the Spanish restaurant in San Rafael featuring flamenco dancers. We missed the show because I needed to go home and nurse myself in bed well before midnight.

Dr. Posner looked at me, waiting.

"I know," I smiled. "Keep talking." Dr. Posner often said this to remind me that I must dig out of my stuck place. By talking and talking and saying one thought that would lead to another, I began to understand why I destroyed good relationships.

"Yes, you got it." His eyes smiled.

"New Year's Eve and my birthday are big deals. Everything feels so significant. I got sick on my birthday once, a long time ago, when a then-boyfriend started hinting about marriage. He took me to The Trident in Sausalito, my favorite restaurant then, for my twenty-sixth birthday.

"It was a strange time when young professional types frequented this seafood restaurant by the bay. Waitresses wore see-through blouses that showed everything. Our server wore a loosely crocheted top with nothing under it. Everyone tried to pretend they weren't looking. It was 1970 in hip Marin County.

"Anyway, I started feeling nauseous and could barely eat. Then, we went to Barry's apartment in San Francisco's Marina

District. He sat on a lounge chair, and I was on the couch facing him when he said maybe we'd get married. I thought he was handsome before then, but suddenly, I felt disgusted, as if I were on the verge of a life with this inadequate, boring person. He'd always been sweet and kind to me. Maybe there was some problem on a deeper level, and we wouldn't have been good together. But I wasn't ready to find out. I withdrew until he gave up on me. He married his next girlfriend."

I paused, and Dr. Posner waited. His expression reminded me to keep talking.

This recollection led me to a more distant one.

"I hardly ever think about this, but I got sick long ago when I was thirteen, at summer camp. This boy liked me, and I liked him in an innocent way; we never even touched. The day before this big, end-of-summer party on the last night of camp, someone told me the boy would give me a locket at the event. I was afraid he'd expect to kiss me. I woke up sick with a stomach ache on the day of the party. I didn't go and never saw him again. So this getting sick thing has happened at least three times," I said.

He nodded.

Then I thought of my mother. "My mother used to get sick physically when some kind of stress was too much for her. She talked about her ulcer when I was growing up and blamed my father for it. She also got sick when the teachers' union voted to strike.

"My mother wanted everyone to like her; choosing either side, to strike or not to, meant making enemies. I remember a couple of times when a strike began; she woke up with a cold and stayed in bed. When she called in sick, she wasn't pretending."

"Nor were you pretending when you got sick on New Year's Eve."

My breathing became even. Dr. Posner didn't give his opinion often, but he was right on the mark, bulls-eye, when he did.

I found myself slowing down, entering a place deep inside myself.

"Yes, I called in sick on New Year's Eve," I whispered, eyes closed, heart open.

46 – Ready

Dad picked me up at Kennedy Airport Friday afternoon in March, wearing a suit instead of his usual post-retirement blue jeans. We drove to New Jersey to join Gloria, Larry, their three children, and a few others for a celebratory dinner at a restaurant to celebrate my niece Rachel's bat mitzvah.

My mother skipped the restaurant dinner and joined us at the synagogue. It would have pained her to sit at a table with my father and strained me to watch them. We could cope in the synagogue, buffered by the crowd and the spacious sanctuary.

As I'd seen in other bar and bat mitzvah ceremonies in Reform synagogues, the rabbi would lift the Torah, a parchment scroll on which a scribe had meticulously written the entire Hebrew Bible. He'd hand it to a grandparent, who'd pass it to a parent, who would give it to the child, so the Torah passed to three generations, symbolizing Jewish continuity.

I sat by my mother in the first row of high-backed oak benches. We watched the rabbi hand the heavy scroll to my father, who carefully passed it to Larry, who gingerly gave it to Rachel, helping her support it by placing his hand under it while she cradled it in her arms. My eyes misted.

My mother's face was pinched. As Dad returned to his place on the bench behind ours, I imagined her thinking, "He gets the spotlight, accepting an honor after leaving me to marry *her*."

Her was Ethel, but my mother never said her name. Ethel boycotted events where my mother, Gloria, or I would be present. Maybe she hadn't wanted reminders that my father had been married before. Possibly, she had lingering hurt feelings from first meeting Gloria and me. Children of divorce are not likely to take an instant liking to their father's new wife. After Dad had introduced us, Gloria and I ignored her over dinner at Lai Fong, one of the usual restaurants we'd gone to with Dad.

My mother's heartaches from the abandonments she suffered—my father's, her father's, and her mother Yetta's—still cut into me deeply. After years of therapy, I could step back and try to separate my life from hers. The words of my opinionated former therapist, Dr. Folger, came to mind as I watched my smiling niece, who had given her speech. She looked small in an oversized upholstered chair beside the rabbi's.

In his inimitable way, Dr. Folger said years earlier, "Don't let her pull that orphanage crap on you." My mother deserved my compassion, but I'd begun to think my life had a chance of evolving differently from her expectations.

After the ceremony, I would stay two nights with Mom in Rockaway; and on Sunday fly to Miami, Florida, for the National Jewish Singles Caribbean Cruise. I'd longed to see the beach again before flying out, so early Sunday morning, I took the short walk to where the boardwalk began, thinking I'd stop there. But as if drawn by a magnet, I continued to the sand, removed my shoes, and walked to the muddy shoreline. My feet tingled as waves touched them.

I gazed at my toes, then out at the waves, some of which crashed beyond where Gloria and I used to bob up and down, rocked by the swells. I glanced at the large expanse of sand and sea, empty except for a few older folks resting on boardwalk benches and a lone walker by the distant shoreline. All were too far away to hear me above the ocean's noise, even if I shouted at the top of my lungs.

I did this as I looked past the waves toward the horizon. I called out to the sea, the sky, and whatever Force would hear me: "I WANT TO GET MARRIED" I smiled and called out: "I'M READY—READY TO GET MARRIED!"

Joy coursed through me. Then tears came. I was crying and smiling and crying. I covered my wet eyes with my hands. Slowing down, I breathed in the fresh, salty air. Calmer, I looked way out into the ocean. I felt an answer emerge from a place far beyond the breakers, beyond where the sea met the sky, beyond time and space, and deep within me:

"YES."

47 – Clowning

1988. Rockaway, New York

My mother drove me to Kennedy Airport. Esther, her friend from their candy-selling days at the orphanage, was in the back seat.

Esther's gray hair sparkled in the sunlight, and her cheeks had a healthy, pink glow. She was aging gracefully. She smiled with interest as my mother talked about her new hobby: clowning.

I wasn't sure about the clown thing; my chest tightened as Mom explained.

"This woman who I met at Clown College—Nancy—we hit it off right away, though she's twenty years younger. Now, we perform at different places. Last month, we entertained children in a pediatric hospital in Brooklyn, and they said they wanted us back. The kids love us, especially when we blow up balloons into animal shapes for them. We perform for free, mostly at hospitals, schools, and senior centers."

"That's nice," I said, uncomfortable about this clown business. "It sounds like you're a hit."

"We sure are," she smiled. "We gave ourselves clown names at the college. She's Fancy Prancin' Nancy, and I'm Dolly Molly. I'm thinking about performing at camp this summer." She meant at Camp Isabella Freedman in Connecticut for active Jewish seniors. My mother was a lifeguard and exercise instructor there.

When the light turned red, she removed a photo from her wallet and handed it to me. "Take a look, sweetie," she said.

Sweetie. I'm still sweetie.

I didn't get this whole thing: my mother, a clown. The photograph showed two stocky clowns. The shorter one's hair was a wild, wooly multicolored wig in shades of green, pink, purple, and orange. She was my mother, in a bright-yellow blouse and a red circle skirt. She looked up at the taller one with a mischievous grin. I wouldn't have recognized her in a crowd.

Nancy, the other clown, towered over my mother in the photo. A black outline around her mouth accented her big clown frown. Both had white-painted faces, a red dot on their noses, and bigger ones on their cheeks. My mother was seventy-five; the make-up hid her age. Nancy wore a bushy, yellow wig, a paisley shirt with a necktie, and big, green polka-dotted pantaloons.

I hoped this phase would soon pass. My mother's clown persona embarrassed me the way I felt as a teenager, seeing her dance around the house. But this was more extreme.

"Your mother is a big kid," said Esther appreciatively.

A big kid. I suddenly saw my mother with new eyes. She was a big kid who loved a good time.

"So, how's your little puppy?" Mom asked, with her eyes on the highway. "Do you have a good place for her while you're away?"

"She's fine. A friend is taking care of her." No point in mentioning David by name. I'd stopped telling her about men in my life long ago. For all my mother knew, I hadn't had a date in over ten years. I'd told her nothing about my conversations with Rabbi Rothstein or the Skolye Rebbe. What good could have come from her knowing I hoped to marry? Or that the cruise I was going on was for Jewish singles?

If my mother had known, she might have hoped I'd meet someone nice. And if I did, she'd ask me later if he was still nice and expect me to say no.

Before I adopted Amie, I'd told my mother I'd been thinking about getting a dog. She said it would be good to "have something warm and cuddly to snuggle with," as though she didn't expect me to marry.

"Nancy and I have a skit about going to Sassoon's Academy in Manhattan for free haircuts by their trainees," she said. "It's based on what happened there years ago. About thirty of us were sitting in the waiting room, hoping for a free cut, but they needed only fifteen. Some weird lady kept calling out in a high-pitched voice: 'Choose me, pleeeaze . . . take me!' I think they picked her so she'd stop."

I'd heard that story before. Lillian, the lady who begged for someone to pick her for a free cut, stayed single and lived a bohemian-artist lifestyle in Greenwich Village. She and my mother became fast friends. Lillian was fifty-nine. Now they sometimes performed together after my mother showed her how to dress and act like a clown.

My mother continued, "I make balloons shaped like dogs and try to bribe Nancy with them because she is acting the part of a Sassoon's trainee who's about to choose a model. At first, she ignores me. She sticks her nose up, prances around, raises her knees high, and stops to point to someone in the audience like she's choosing them."

"Sounds terrific, Mom," I said, forcing a smile. I'm not fond of clown acts, but I didn't want to hurt her feelings.

"Your mother is so creative," Esther said. "She used to invent dances and choreograph performances at the Academy. People still talk about her Rope Dance."

I turned to her, nodding and smiling politely. "Yes, I know."

Once my shy adolescence passed, I learned to relax and enjoy dancing. Probably, I'd get in some dancing on the cruise; there'd be a party every night.

Like my mother, I can't talk and drive simultaneously without missing an occasional turnoff. Esther helped, pointing out signs along the way. "We're almost there," she said. "Just take the next exit, Mollie."

"Thanks, Esther. Good thing you came along." She looked straight ahead and drove at her usual slow pace, paying attention to signs.

"Marcia, you'd like clown college," my mother said as we neared the airport. "You'll have fun, and with your artistic talent, you'll be great with the make-up and costume. You'll make people laugh and forget their troubles. Everybody loves a clown.

"I can give you some ideas for your clown acts. We're working on a new one where I pretend I think Prancing Nancy is a horse. I'll try to climb on her back to ride her. The kids will hoot and holler. The youngest ones will probably yell, 'Stop! She's not really a horse.'"

She turned to me briefly and added, "You could put together a similar act."

"Sure, Mom," I said, hoping my sarcasm escaped her, but I'd reached my limit. I felt guilty for behaving this way toward my mother, who loved me more than anyone else ever did or would.

At the passenger drop-off curb, I leaned over to kiss her goodbye. I realized I'd miss her. My eyes moistened as I hugged her.

"Take good care of yourself, Marcia," she said. And then, "I almost forgot," as she dug a few long skinny balloons out of her purse. "Take these to practice on. In no time, you'll be able to blow them up and twist them into animal shapes."

"Thanks, Mom." I shoved them into my purse and left the photo of the two clowns on the front seat.

On my way to the gate, I already missed her and wished I could see her more often. Still, I was relieved to be on my own again. It was difficult for me to resist getting sucked into how she defined me. My mother told me to live my life as she lived hers, like I was supposed to want what she wanted: "Be a teacher,"

"Take up tap dancing," and "Be a clown." Denying her felt like defying her.

My mother was wrong to want me to be a clown, dress in a costume, and act the part. Suddenly, I understood why my aversion to wearing costumes had grown stronger lately. I did not want to pretend to be someone else. I had been in hiding for so long.

Why make it even harder to find me?

48 – Caribbean Cruise

1988. The Caribbean

Blessed are You, Lord our G-d, King of the universe,
Who opens the eyes of the blind.
— A blessing in the Jewish prayer book

Jen and I were cabin mates on the cruise. She was a quiet twenty-seven-year-old from Wisconsin with a sweet face and pixie haircut. We compared notes after the first night's party in the Captain's Lounge.

"Most of these guys seem to be looking for a good time, and there are enough women here who will throw themselves at them," Jen said, "but not me." I nodded in agreement. "There are twice as many women as men here, so the guys can pick and choose. We'll have a good time anyway. Do you like to snorkel?"

"I love snorkeling."

When we turned off the lights, it was pitch black. I slept soundly each night, rocked by the waves like a baby in a cradle, and woke up refreshed in the morning.

Jen and I became fast friends. We snorkeled in Cozumel and Grand Cayman Island. I merged blissfully into an underwater world among exotic tropical fish of all the rainbow colors.

In Jamaica, we took a taxi to a famous waterfall through which we walked on slippery rocks, emerging happily soaked. We bought straw hats in Haiti's large covered market.

Jen accepted the persistent attentions of a fresh-faced, kind man about her age she'd met at the Captain's party. He came to pick her up for the evening's entertainment and didn't seem to mind when I sat with them at dinner or a show. Jen and I talked a lot during our outings and in the cabin. I must have mentioned David a couple of times.

Meanwhile, people were pairing off. I saw them dining together, trying their luck in the ship's casino, and sitting companionably at evening programs. A few might even evolve into "we-met-on-the-cruise" marriages. I couldn't help feeling a little sorry for myself. Why hadn't I met anyone?

I'd received little attention from men on the cruise, except George, a chunky, cynical guy in his late thirties who often hung around the casino. He'd attempted a pass "because that's how it is on the ship," he explained when I rolled my eyes. After I laughed off his remark, he conversed with me like a pal when our paths crossed.

This wasn't George's first time on this cruise. "Are you coming again next year?" He asked me. Without missing a beat, I said, "I expect to be married by this time next year."

Astonished, I'd done a double-take. That was *me* sounding confident about marrying soon, and I was perfectly sane. Although I had no particular person in mind, my snappy comeback wasn't banter.

George raised his eyebrows, surprised.

On the morning of the last day of the cruise, I stretched out on a lounge chair on a quiet deck. As I opened my novel, I remembered something Jen said after her young man had walked her to our cabin and said good night.

"He really likes you," I'd said. "You barely encourage him, and he keeps coming back." She smiled half-heartedly. She didn't mind letting him escort her around the ship but didn't want any-thing more. "Well, at least *you* have someone paying attention to you; I haven't met anyone," I moped.

"That's because you're emotionally committed to David," she said.

What? I shrugged off the thought, letting it float away like a fish drifting out of sight into a coral reef.

A bit later, another woman I'd met earlier said nearly the same thing. She was an attractive attorney from Berkeley, California, in her mid-fifties. As we chatted over fresh-squeezed orange juice and croissants at the ship's outdoor café, she said, "I haven't met anyone, but that's because of my age," she said. "But I'm enjoy-ing the vacation, and I've met some nice women. But you've probably met lots of men," she said, looking around at clusters of men and women at other tables. "You're the right age."

"The guys must not have noticed. I've been feeling invisi-ble all week."

"I'm surprised," she said. "You're one of the most attractive women on the cruise." She looked puzzled, as though trying to figure me out.

I felt a warm glow inside.

While on my second croissant with my attorney friend, she looked into my eyes and said, "I think you haven't met anyone because you're already attached, probably to the guy taking care of your dog. You must be sending out 'unavailable' signals."

My jaw dropped. I felt a slight quiver inside as I put down my juice glass, nearly spilling its contents.

"Do you really think so?" I asked.

That conversation was still in my head when I put my book on the deck and turned on my stomach to bask in the sun's warmth. I closed my eyes and wondered, *What is going on with me that I need near-strangers to tell me what I'm feeling and where I'm heading?*

The dull ache I'd connected to feeling invisible was gone. *I must love David*, I realized, and that felt fine.

49 – Marriage Minded

1988. San Rafael, California

David and I shared a pesto pizza at the Brooklyn Pizzeria a week later. The lunch rush was over; it was just us and an older couple seated across the room. Sunlight streamed through slatted blinds, casting bright stripes on our table.

I relaxed against our booth's red vinyl upholstery, bracing myself for "the talk." Regardless of how he'd respond, I'd be okay because I knew I would marry—David or someone else. I hoped it would be him, but if not, I'd move on.

"We've been seeing each other for a while," I said, watching his unguarded expression. "I'm wondering where you want this to go . . ."

He hesitated for a moment. "I don't know," he said. "I'll need to know if I'm ready."

"When will you know?"

"In two weeks." Nothing in David's manner suggested he felt trapped. I gathered he'd already begun thinking about a future with me.

Two weeks. I nodded and smiled to myself. I'd have given him a month. The aroma of sizzling mozzarella, tomato sauce, and garlic wafted our way as the cook slid a pizza from the oven. We turned to follow its presentation to the other couple.

Returning to David, I said, "Okay."

I watched his handsome profile as we drove back to my place. He noticed and flashed his shy smile at me. *He's so open and sincere.*

If David said he wanted to marry me, I planned to give him an escape hatch. At times, I felt guilty about not having told him my secret. But I stuck to my decision: If he said he wanted marriage, that's when I would tell him. I followed Dr. Posner's advice to avoid revealing my psychiatric past to anyone not ready to marry me. Enough people had stigmatized me; why risk more hurt for no good reason?

I scrunched in the passenger seat. My upper arms pressed into my rib cage as though trying to squeeze myself into nothingness. I glanced at David as we approached the hill to my condo. *How would he feel about my having been locked up for being crazy?* I never trusted any man as much as him. If kind, easygoing David didn't accept the real me, who would?

So absorbed was I in these thoughts, I didn't realize he'd parked until he said, "We're home, sweetie."

I relaxed a bit and smiled. *Sweetie. I hope you'll always call me that.*

A few days later, on a Saturday night, David made no move to leave the car after we returned from a movie. After an evening out, we'd often stayed in his car's cozy darkness, where it was harder to see and easier to speak freely.

David turned toward me and said, "About what we were talking about last Sunday, I've thought it over and . . ."

After less than one week. I took a deep breath to center myself. The streetlight cast a gleam on the steering wheel.

"I'm ready." Even in the dark, I saw he was beaming.

He's ready! "That's wonderful," I said. As he leaned to hold me tightly, I loved feeling his arms around me and hugged him back. Then a voice inside me said, *slow down.* I gently released myself.

"I need to tell you something. I hope it won't change any-thing," I said, "but in case it does, I want you to know . . ."

I breathed in and out slowly and stared at the ray of light on the steering wheel. "This is hard to talk about and too sensitive for me to have told you before." I paused to steady my shaky voice.

"More than ten years ago, I had a very difficult time. I became psychotic and was hospitalized. It happened two more times. The third time, I started taking lithium. I still take it. I've been fine since then, except for a fluke when I went on a salt-free diet a few years ago." I turned to David and explained, "Lithium needs salt to work."

He listened, taking it in.

"I understand this might make you feel different," I said, with a catch in my voice. "You may want more time to think it over."

"I had no idea," he said softly, looking straight ahead. "What an ordeal."

I tried to read his face. I imagined he was stunned, that even hearing about it was an ordeal for him.

"I think I need a week to process this."

I nodded. I could handle that. The worst thing would have been for David to have said it made no difference, and after marrying me, to realize that it did.

"That's fine," I said.

During the next few days, I feared becoming anxious and panicky about what David might have been thinking. I coped by keeping busy.

The marketing director of an international shipping com-pany wanted small, leather-bound world atlases on which to imprint the firm's logo. None of the advertising specialty distrib-utors courting her business knew where to find them—except me. I'd recently picked up a sample of one at an industry trade show in Texas.

I drove into San Francisco to show it to her. On Tuesday, I instructed the factory to imprint a thousand to drop-ship to her, anticipating my biggest profit. Thinking about this helped keep my mind off David.

David called Wednesday night. "Would you like to go for a picnic on Saturday at Golden Gate Park?" he asked. "Maybe take out a paddleboat."

Golden Gate Park. That's where David said his father proposed to his mother. My eyes misted. I closed them and smiled.

50 – The Chocolate-Vanilla Solution

1988. Greenbrae, California

"I'm engaged," I told my mother on the phone.

"It's a miracle." She probably thought I'd stopped dating long ago.

When I called my father, Ethel answered. "I'm so excited for you," she said, and "I'll have your father call you as soon as he gets home. I'll let you be the one to tell him."

"I'm so happy," said my father. After a brief pause, "You know, I can't help thinking . . . maybe the divorce had something to do with it being so hard for you."

Brilliant, Dad, like I hadn't figured that out some time ago. But I loved my father and was glad he was happy for me.

My friend Eileen, who'd been there when I met David, said, "That's wonderful. You beat the odds. You know it was in the newspaper: a woman over forty who never married has about as much chance of getting married as being run over by a truck—"

"I know," I said. *Thanks, Eileen.*

David flew to New York to meet my mother in person and talked to my father on the phone. "Because I wanted them to know the man their daughter was marrying was okay," he said. I felt moved by how sweet and thoughtful David was to do this.

I had an idea about the marriage ceremony that seemed too far-fetched to mention to David—a Chabad wedding. I attended one at the Rothstein's home three months earlier. I'd never seen anything like it and loved it.

In a modest, long-sleeved white gown, the bride, or *kallah*, sat on a chair adorned with oversized bows, lace, and ribbons in a room filled with women before the ceremony. The groom gave a scholarly presentation on the Torah to the men in a different room. Next, two of them escorted him to the bride. He covered her face with the veil. Then, the men brought him outside to the chuppah.

Chani and another woman, carrying lit candles, walked the bride to the chuppah, one on each side of her. The three of them circled the groom seven times to symbolize she would make a home for him and protect him.

The sense of joy mingled with holiness was palpable. With everything done precisely according to Jewish law, the foundation of their marriage felt rock solid.

I told myself this was the wedding I wanted, but I pushed the thought away. I wasn't like these people. I didn't keep kosher and only observed the Sabbath that one time.

So I set up a wedding date at Rodef Shalom, ordered invitations, and began arranging for a caterer. David and I were planning food offerings for the reception when we had our first argument. I'd spread some lists of possible choices on my dining table. Among other selections, we decided on a princess cake with pale-green marzipan frosting.

I said, "I want us to have a Chabad wedding."

"What do you mean you want a Chabad wedding? We already decided to do it at Rodef Shalom."

"I know, but I want Rabbi Rothstein to marry us. I feel connected to him. He understands me."

"My family and friends won't be comfortable at an Orthodox wedding. They don't live that way, and neither do we."

"So they're more important than me? Are we getting married for them?" Impatient, I closed my eyes. How could I explain to David that anything less than the real thing would feel shallow?

"I'm a Reform Jew."

"So am I, basically, but—"

"Their ceremony is sexist, the way they make the woman walk around and around the man—"

"You've never been to a Hasidic wedding. It feels so meaningful."

David stared at the bookcase, stone-faced.

"Besides, *I'm* the one who circles *you*. If I don't mind, why should you?"

"My elderly cousin, Ruth. After she flies here from Florida—she'll be horrified."

"Maybe you're right, but I can't let go of wanting Rabbi Rothstein to marry us."

I'd never seen David so impermeable. He wouldn't budge, and I couldn't blame him, especially after I'd arranged for the Reform wedding.

I admired David for wanting his family and friends to feel comfortable. He had a point. How would our assimilated Jewish and non-Jewish family members and friends mix with a bearded rabbi in a black fedora and black frock coat who spoke with a Yiddish accent? And there would be strange rituals and customs, such as a heavily veiled me walking in a circle around David seven times. Would they refuse to participate in the joyous dancing because men and women do it in separate circles?

Rabbi Rothstein and others in his community were the first people I knew who expected me to marry. Their faith in me boosted my confidence.

Another person believed in me that way—the Skolye Rebbe from Brooklyn. *You can phone me anytime.*

I knew that in the old country, Jews consulted rabbis about their problems. Hadn't I done the same in talking with Rabbi Rothstein and the Skolye Rebbe, who'd said, "I remember everything"?

On a Wednesday afternoon seven weeks before our Reform wedding date, I phoned the Skolye Rebbe. After I described David's and my conflict, he said, "David is sincere. He's not Orthodox. He is who he is. You want different things. One likes chocolate and the other vanilla. So have both."

"It's okay to have two weddings?"

"Just have the Orthodox one first."

When David came over that evening, we discussed the two-wedding solution.

"Okay," he said. "But I don't want to spoil it for my relatives flying in from the East Coast for the Reform wedding. I don't want them to know we've already had a ceremony. Also, I want the government's document, the marriage certificate, to have the date of the Reform wedding."

At ten o'clock that night, we phoned Rabbi Rothstein to say we wanted him to marry us.

"What about the Reform wedding?"

"We'll have that too."

"Come right over."

We sat at Rabbi Rothstein's dining room table half an hour later. He said, "Let's do it this Sunday, June 12th. I'll arrange for a minyan. I need to know your Hebrew names."

David's English name is his Hebrew name. But I wasn't given a Hebrew name. A complex discussion ensued. At some point, I mentioned that my middle name is Naomi.

"Why didn't you say so? Your Hebrew name is *Naomi*," said Rabbi Rothstein.

Chani lent me a dress from her collection for future brides, bargains she'd picked up over time. The one that fit was a gauzy, white gown with a ruffle at the neck, too fluffy for my taste but good enough for a wedding on four days' notice.

When I phoned my mother, hoping she might come to my Chabad wedding on short notice, she said, "Those men don't think I'm good enough to shake my hand. I'll see you next month." She knew Orthodox Jewish men do not touch women in most situations, but she didn't understand why. Given the amount of intrusive touching women experience, myself included, I'm okay with this prohibition as a "fence" that guards against inappropriate touching.

My father said, "I'm coming," astonishing me.

Eileen said she'd come. "I'm willing to put up with that for the sake of our friendship."

David and I picked up kosher cold cuts, salads, and drinks. Chani made a sheet cake. On Sunday, about twenty-five people attended our small, beautiful Hasidic wedding in the home of Rabbi Yisrael Rice, assistant to Rabbi Rothstein.

I sat in the decorated chair, and David covered my face with the veil. He wore a kittel, a white robe traditionally worn by a Jewish man on his wedding day, and I'd never seen him look more handsome.

Rabbi Rothstein explained that the groom breaks the glass after the marriage is finalized to remind us of the destruction of the Temple in Jerusalem, even in our happiest times. Before the festive meal, the men and women danced in separate circles on the backyard lawn. Rabbi Rice, who had gymnastic skills, in keeping with the tradition to "delight the bride," did a series of flips.

Six weeks later, we had a Reform wedding in the temple's sanctuary, followed by a catered luncheon in its courtyard for a hundred and fifty guests. My mother flew in early enough to join David, me, and David's Florida cousin, Ruth, for lunch at a restaurant. My mother carried a knapsack, and Ruth said, "Your mother's like a girl scout."

Chocolate and vanilla. The Skolye Rebbe's advice was brilliant. Everyone was happy. My father said he liked our Chabad wedding better because "it was more *haimish*."

David and me on our Reform wedding day.

51 – Stopping Lithium

1991. Berkeley, California

When I married at forty-three and was trying to become pregnant, Dr. Posner urged me to stop taking lithium because it could harm the fetus. Petrified to go off it, I recalled the revolving door of psychiatric patients from my San Francisco General Hospital job. Many, like Jackie, returned each time they stopped taking their medication.

I'd been doing fine on lithium. I shuddered, embarrassed by my past bizarre behavior at my executive director job, witnessed by my staff and probably relayed to board members. I pictured myself strapped to a table where they injected a tranquilizer that sedated me into a barely conscious, catatonic-like state. Six months later, I lost that job, which had become my identity. *What havoc might I wreak if I stopped taking lithium now?*

But I wanted a baby, and I trusted Dr. Posner. He suggested a two-week trial off the drug, preceded by a session with David present. David agreed to monitor my behavior in case I needed to resume taking lithium. Still frightened, I began the two-week vacation from lithium.

During this trial period, I asked David to get good seats for *The Phantom of the Opera* in San Francisco. He said, "I'll see what I can do."

On the night of the performance, I wore the same, happy, red dress I'd worn the night David and I first met. Its bright color and swirly skirt made me feel vibrant. But as the young usher led us up the stairs of the theater's huge orchestra section, higher and higher, I began to churn inside. My resentment peaked when she led us to the last row.

I was fuming. As the usher handed us programs, I looked at her and half-joked, "This is what it's like to be married." She laughed, and I felt some of my tension release.

Back home that night, David said my comment to the usher might mean I was becoming manic.

Oh, noooo.

"Here we go again," I said to Dr. Posner. "I get just a bit free about expressing myself, maybe embarrass David a little, and suddenly I'm C-R-A-Z-Y. I want to see what I did as *healthy*. I aired my feelings instead of holding them in." I was annoyed with David, but could he have been right? I felt too insecure to trust my judgment. I'd done that before and ended up in hospitals.

I waited anxiously for Dr. Posner's verdict: "If that's the only thing that happened that was unusual, I am not concerned."

Whew!

The two experimental weeks passed without further incident. Amazed and relieved, I didn't go back on lithium, though it waited in my medicine cabinet for a long time, just in case.

52 – Arnold

1991. San Rafael, California, and Rockaway, New York

Letters mentioning Arnold arrived in my mother's loopy script. I expected him to be another link in a chain of unstable or otherwise unsuitable men she'd dated occasionally since divorcing.

Who is this Arnold? I wondered when his name kept appearing in my mother's correspondence. "Arnold and I went to his nephew's son's Bar Mitzvah in New Jersey. His nephew works for the Post Office delivering mail; he's a sweet guy. I met a couple of his nieces; one lives in Florida."

In another, she wrote, "Arnold's daughter, her husband, and their two children (four and seven years old) came to Rockaway on Sunday. Gloria joined us. We had lunch at the house. I kept it simple—sliced cold turkey with bread for sandwiches and potato salad. After, we all walked down to the boardwalk. The kids are cute and well-behaved. They got a big kick taking off their shoes and splashing in the water up to their ankles. Maybe I'll teach them to swim when it gets warm next summer. Start with the elementary backstroke. We'll see."

My mother seemed to be becoming a part of Arnold's family, whoever he was. Finally, I phoned and asked, "Who's Arnold?"

"You might remember him—the arts and crafts director at camp Isabella Freedman, where we both still work every summer? When you visited two years ago, I introduced you to him, his wife, and the others at the table where we ate." I drew a blank. "She was very sick. He was devoted to her. He gave her all his attention until she died over a year ago. He never said a word to me in her presence.

"Last summer, he was withdrawn and still barely spoke to me. Then, in September, we both attended a gathering in Manhattan for the camp staff. He and I talked; one thing led to another and—"

"And what?"

"I was going to call tonight to tell you. We're going to get married."

My mouth dropped open. "You're getting married!"

"Yes, three weeks from Sunday. I don't expect you to come all the way out here for the ceremony—"

"I'm coming. Of course, I want to be there. I think David will, too."

"We'll have the ceremony at the house with Rabbi Weiss. Poor guy. His wife died not long ago. She suffered for a long time. He's still the rabbi at West End Temple after all these years. He's been through a lot with her; maybe it was rough on her being the wife of a rabbi—"

"Just a minute, Mom." The impossible was happening, and my mother was off on a tangent. I had to ask, "How did you decide . . . after all these years, when it seemed like you didn't want to get married again?"

"I wasn't thinking about a wedding, but Arnold insisted."

After we said goodbye, I called Gloria.

"He seems like a nice guy," Gloria said. "His family is working class. They talk differently from us, down-to-earth. They seem to look up to Mom because of her education and her having been a teacher. They revere Arnold. He's probably helped some of them out at crucial times. They love Mom and are very happy for him.

"It's been pretty quick, though—only about three or four months of seeing a lot of each other. But I suppose at their age, there's not much point of waiting too long—"

"Maybe you're right," I said. "I hope so."

"I just hope she knows what she's doing. I talked to Lillian the other day. She and Mom talked over tea after performing a recent clown show at a Manhattan hospital. Mom said when she tried to reach out to Arnold last summer at camp, he shooed her away. But something changed later, and he started liking her."

"So the romance started to blossom in September?"

"I guess. They're the same age, seventy-eight. Arnold was a furrier before he retired. He learned the trade in Brazil. He escaped there after fleeing Germany in the 1930s."

Mom and Arnold

"Maybe he was still mourning for his wife during the summer. How do they look together?"

"They look sweet. And happy. He gazes at her a lot, sort of beams. He's a bit taller than Mom, mostly bald with some wisps of hair, and they're both a little on the plump side. It's like Lillian said about Mom," Gloria sighed. "'At her age, there are hardly any men left, and she gets them all.'"

After we hung up, I shook my head and smiled at the thought of my mother as a live wire.

She was the last person I expected to marry again. But Arnold was different from other men who passed through her life. She had seen how he treated his invalid wife at the camp staff's big, round dining table for three summers. Unlike her father, Morris, my father, and men she'd dated post-divorce, Arnold came with a guarantee. He'd proven himself a mensch who had stuck by his wife no matter what.

I wondered if my marriage to David helped my mother take another chance on marriage. She adored David and defended him when I complained. "He often wears pants that show dirt. Sometimes there's a hole in them and his socks. When I tell him, he shrugs his shoulders as if to say, what's the big deal?"

"You're lucky to be married to him," my mother said. "I'll never forget when he flew to New York after you got engaged, just to meet me and make sure I approved."

David often spoke to her on the phone from California after she and I finished talking. He showed interest in her activities, listening patiently.

She never asked me, "Is he still nice?"

I imagined my mother thinking, "If Marcia can succeed at marriage—and she's not the easiest person to live with . . ."

I felt a giddy happiness. First me, now her. We were reversing the tide. A couple of days before the wedding, my mother and I went to Yolanda's, a women's clothing shop on Beach 116th Street, to find her an outfit for the big day. Mom knew the owner and sometimes shopped there. She tried on several things, but none looked right. It was my idea for us to shop; I think Mom went to humor me. But she didn't want to disappoint Yolanda. "I could use a bra," she said and bought one.

When we arrived for the wedding, it was misty outside. My mother stood surrounded by a small crowd in her living room. She wore a bright red skirt, a matching jacket trimmed with black lace around the border, and a confident smile. A band around her forehead secured a homemade veil of loosely woven black mesh. She looked like a flamenco dancer, but somehow it worked.

Arnold's round face beamed above his dignified gray business suit with a white carnation on the lapel.

"Marcia!" my mother said. As we hugged, I took care not to squish her corsage. "I won't kiss you," she whispered, "I don't want to get lipstick on you." She glanced at David and said, "I'm thrilled you could both come."

"We wouldn't miss it," he said. "You're a beautiful bride, Mollie." She looked down; I sensed her blushing under her rouge. Turning to Arnold, David said, "We're so glad to meet you finally." Seeing Arnold looking so ready to marry thrilled and jolted me. My mother, a bride!

"Yes, we are," I added. "We've heard so many wonderful things about you. I hope you and Mom will be very happy." I sensed shyness in Arnold's eyes and his soft smile. I liked him.

While we waited for Rabbi Weiss, who was late, I wandered into the kitchen, where I found Esther, Mom's old friend. A puffy cloud of white hair surrounded her joyous pink face. I gave her a hello kiss, and she started talking excitedly.

"This is wonderful," Esther said, handing me a mail-order catalog featuring knick-knacks like flower pots, small shelf units, and novelty salt and pepper shakers. "I order from them all the time. The more you buy, the more you save. Look at the back cover. There, that's it." It showed how the discount increased with each additional fifty dollars' worth of merchandise ordered. "So I keep buying and saving! You might want to do this too. I can tell them to send you a catalog."

I stared at her. Esther's small Forest Hills apartment overflowed with books stacked on the floor because there was no more shelf space. My mother's intellectual friend was senile and wasting her teachers' pension on junk.

Her husband, Bernie, caught my eye and rolled both of his.

"But, Esther, the *more* you spend, the *less* money you have left," I reasoned.

"Don't you understand? I'm *saving*," she said as if explaining the obvious to a small child.

Bernie shook his head to signal: Don't bother; she's too far gone.

I forced a smile, holding back tears until I reached the bathroom.

Rabbi Weiss arrived. He'd been waiting at the synagogue, either because he'd forgotten that the wedding would be at the house, or my mother hadn't told him.

He conducted a simple, dignified ceremony, starting with, "I've known Mollie for nearly forty years." After he pronounced the couple husband and wife, everyone applauded. As we ate deli-style sandwiches and pastries, I sat near Arnold's niece, an attractive woman in her forties. "My uncle is so happy," she said. "He's a wonderful person. I wouldn't miss his wedding."

I met Arnold's nephew on my way to the kitchen for a cream soda. He was about fifty, divorced, and lived in New Jersey. "I work for the Postal Service," he said, "but I'm tired of it. I'm looking for something different, maybe start a business." I liked his sincerity and felt like he viewed me as family.

Arnold's daughter, Marcia, was petite and pixie-like, with a quick smile and a thick New York accent. We joked about sharing the same name while she attended to her three young children, wanting to be sure the food on paper plates went nowhere except in their mouths. Her brother Joel, tall with gray hair, said, "Your mother is wonderful. Because of her, my father has woken up and come alive again."

"It's sad to see Esther's not herself anymore," my mother said. She and Arnold sat on the couch. "But at least she has Bernie to take care of her. I told you how they met when he was a struggling artist ten years younger than she is. She supported him all those years because he never really earned much. He drove a taxi now and then. He's devoted to her, so she'll be okay.

"Did I ever tell you how Esther and I met when I was selling candy at the Academy? I had a dream job for a nine-year-old. One day I wanted to take a break just when Esther came by and—"

"Excuse me, Mom," I said, fearing she would drive Arnold batty with her endless monologues. "Those lovely women I met from your senior center are near the door with their coats. I'm going to say goodbye to them. Do you want to come with me?" The crowd had thinned out noticeably.

As she started to rise, Arnold smiled contentedly and said, "I can listen to your mother for hours."

He found her fascinating! This was truly a made-in-heaven match.

"Never mind," I said to my mother, smiling and motioning for her to sit. "I'll tell them goodbye for both of us."

53 – Saying Goodbye

1991. Rockaway, New York

The party wound down, and Mom and Arnold looked tired. They held hands on the living room couch.

David phoned the car service to drive us to the airport. When I told my mother we were leaving, she said, "So soon?" her eyelids drooping with fatigue. She released Arnold's hand and told him she'd be in the kitchen. "I'll pack a few leftovers to take on the plane."

"That's okay, Mom. Please stay here and relax. Thanks anyway. The driver will be here any minute."

She looked at me as though puzzled, then at Arnold and shrugged. I imagined her thinking, *It is so hard to have a daughter who rejects food.* But she smiled.

Looking through the vestibule's glass panes, I saw that the mist had changed to a heavy drizzle. It was getting dark; the rain made it almost black outside.

My mother pressed a Waldbaum's shopping bag into my hand. It weighed a ton.

"So you won't get hungry on the plane."

"Thanks, Mom. I love you." I hugged her.

"The driver's here," David said. We have to leave *right now*." He smiled at my mother and Arnold. "I wish you both a wonderful life together. We'll talk soon."

"Me too," I said. "Bye, Mom. Bye, Arnold." I felt flustered, not wanting to leave.

"I'll take good care of your mother, don't worry," said Arnold. "Have a safe trip."

I hugged my mother again and held her for an extra beat, not wanting to let go. My eyes moistened. *Don't let her see you cry. Be happy for her. Let her remember you that way.*

Rain splashed the windshield as we headed toward Kennedy Airport. I thought of my mother, looking superb, smiling before and after the ceremony, and appropriately serious during it. Her red outfit was more *her* than anything at Yolanda's. She'd probably known she'd wear clothes that looked like a flamenco dancer's and were already in her closet.

Arnold would be good for her. I pictured his gentle face. I felt buoyed remembering the whirl of conversations at the wedding and my pleasure in seeing Gloria and my niece and nephews; the older two were in their teens. Seeing my mother's old childhood friend from the orphanage, Esther, whom I loved, was bitter-sweet. Who would have guessed she'd become senile at seventy-eight?

Esther reminded me of the saying: *we're all on borrowed time.* Who knew when anyone's state, including our own, might change from mental or physical soundness to what we never dreamed would happen?

When she was young and in love with Morris, my grandmother, Yetta, could not have imagined how her life would unfold. My mother, once adored by my father, hadn't believed he'd ever leave her.

As for me, I never expected to land in a psychiatric ward and be forced to ingest drugs that turned me into a near-zombie. When that did happen, I was sure that the whole mess had been a fluke until later events proved me wrong.

Most of us want to believe we have a guarantee against suffering and are stunned to learn otherwise. *Carpe diem.*

I like my mother's wise, straightforward advice: *Find happiness every day. Store up the good times to shore you up during the rough ones.* Somewhere along the way, my mother transformed her challenges into lessons and a philosophy to live by.

Seated beside David, waiting to board the plane, I unwrapped a sandwich from the Waldbaum's bag and inhaled the mouth-watering aroma. *Thanks, Mom.* Pastrami on rye, New York style, with coleslaw and mustard. Just how I liked it.

Afterword

My mother and Arnold had a wonderful marriage, cherishing and supporting each other through health and sickness. Mom taught Arnold the ins and outs of clowning, and they performed together. Both continued to work in the summer at camps for Jewish seniors: Arnold as the arts and crafts counselor and Mom as the lifeguard. During other seasons, they enjoyed activities at Rockaway's senior centers.

Theirs was a real-life, happily-ever-after story; real life because no couple is delighted with each other constantly. Once, Arnold became so annoyed with my mother that he stayed in his Brooklyn apartment for two days. Gloria called it a lovers' quarrel and helped patch things up. My mother's next-door neighbor, Mary, told me, "Arnold is so patient; he waits in the car for your mother when they're going somewhere."

Like mother, like daughter, I often run late, finding one more thing to do and then another while David *usually* waits patiently in the car. After being married to Arnold for a while, Mom said, "Life is better in pairs."

Mom passed away in March 2000. Arnold survived her by a couple of years.

About my grandmother, Yetta Herman, did she have a mental illness for the rest of her life? Or had she experienced a breakdown because of her overwhelmingly stressful situation? If her condition was chronic, could she have been treated as an outpatient with lithium or another drug, had such remedies been available in 1913? Would her fate have been different if mental health and social welfare programs like today's existed back then?

David and I have been married for over thirty-five years. We're blessed to have each other and to be parents of Avi, our now-adult son. When the Skolye Rebbe told me to expect a ninety-seven percent happy marriage, I was disappointed because my expectations were fairytale-like and perfectionistic. Now I know that even in the happiest marriages, there are differences to accept, tolerate, or work around.

During my episodes, some of the "real me" surfaced. Some dreams I voiced have come true. When I was manic, my psyche seemed to be dealing with my hidden desires to run a family counseling center, adopt a dog, get married, and become a mother. Subsequently, I became the executive director of a family service agency, got a dog, married, and became a mother.

2024. What Madness Might Mean, and a Cautionary Note

Did the anger workshop in 1974 release something in me that needed expression? The release may have helped my growth, but could it have happened without sending me over the edge, missing my sister's wedding, and spending eight days in a drug-induced stupor in an awful psych ward?

Modern psychology has debunked the idea, popular in the 1970s, that beating on pillows and other objects and screaming out our anger are good things to do. It can be exhilarating and cathartic to act out our anger. But these practices can imply permission to vent anger impulsively and dramatically. Research has shown that these so-called therapeutic practices increase aggression and damage relationships, which happened to me.

About my manic episodes, I had a delusion during each one that I was about to marry someone who hadn't committed to me. Had I needed marriage to fix my brain chemistry? According to Jewish teachings, the souls of a wife and husband become one when they marry. Was my soul insisting that I unite with its other half? After settling into a good marriage, I learned I no longer needed medicine to stay sane. Did marriage cure my bipolar disorder? Or would I have outgrown the illness even if I hadn't married? I think my marriage was responsible, but there is no definite way to know.

There's an element of mystery about what causes mental illness. Who knows what changed my brain chemistry so that I stopped needing lithium? Everyone needs to find their own meaning.

But I want to caution anyone thinking of altering or discontinuing a psychotropic drug: I strongly urge you to follow the recommendation of the physician or other knowledgeable professional who prescribes and carefully monitors your medication. There have been disastrous results for too many mentally ill people who decided to discontinue a potentially life-saving medication without medical supervision.

Another point I want to emphasize: We are all much bigger and more complex than any diagnosis. We cannot prevent all judging and stigmatizing. However, by sharing our stories, I hope we help reduce the stigma around mental illness. I yearn for a time when people will extend similar acceptance of and compassion to people who have a mental illness as we give to those with a physical one.

Theories abound about what causes mental illnesses. We continue to learn.

Acknowledgments

My mother said a long time ago, "You will write my memoirs" [*sic*]; she didn't ask. Maybe she believed I owed her this because she grew up in an orphanage, and I didn't. But I felt uneasy about her expectation and guilty for not agreeing. Why wouldn't she write them herself? But after all she'd been through, how could I disappoint her?

This book is my memoir. I've included some of my mother's story and her mother's. Some details about my grandmother are true. Most are imagined, based on the little I know about her life. Much intertwining exists between my mother's life and mine. So, it seems I'm granting a bit of her wish to write her memoirs after all—and I am grateful to her for telling me as a child that I could succeed in almost any path in life I chose to pursue.

Publishing this book was not an easy decision, however. How could I switch from treating my psychiatric history as a guarded secret to sharing it with the world? I feared that my openness would make me relive the stigmatization and shame I endured over forty years ago. Would colleagues and associates lose their respect for me? Would some friends ghost me, as I had experienced before?

My main reason for considering "coming out" was to show that someone with a mental illness is much bigger and more complex than their diagnosis. And so I am grateful to everyone who encouraged me to publish this memoir. These include beta readers David Berger, Linda Bloom, Francine Falk-Allen, Adrian Fried, Amy Kahn, Leslie Marks, Carol Olicker, and Marian Sanders.

I appreciate Marian Sanders and Carol Olicker, both named above, and Eileen Olicker. Their support sustained me when working in a hostile environment decades ago was a daily challenge for me. All remain treasured friends.

The outspoken psychiatrist, whom I call Dr. Folger in this book, deserves two huge thank yous. One is for maintaining me on a much lower amount of lithium than the widely accepted level. His decision may have prevented me from experiencing kidney damage, tremors, and other damaging side effects of lithium that caused it to no longer be prescribed routinely for bipolar disorder.

I also thank Dr. Folger for his response when I approached him at a cultural event a few years ago, after he'd retired. He was still mentally sharp. I wasn't surprised that he didn't remember me. But I thought he would after I said I'd been hospitalized three times for manic-depression, omitting the salt-free glitch. He looked blank. I appreciate him for letting me know I wasn't so strange.

Writers' groups are an antidote to loneliness and slacking off. I value mine immensely. Francine Falk-Allen has led the "Just Write" meet-up group for over a decade. Leslie Marks and I have been meeting on Sunday mornings for even longer. Lori Ahazarian coordinates my Wednesday group.

I appreciate editor Mary Neighbour and her team at MediaNeighbours. Mary has been terrific at clearing out the manuscript's clutter, improving the organization of its chapters, and suggesting changes for more clarity. And she is an absolute pleasure to work with.

Finally, beyond words, I appreciate my husband, David Berger, for his unwavering support for my writing, being my loving life partner, and so much more. He strongly encouraged me to publish this book despite my reservations.

Glossary

bentch. A Yiddish word meaning to say a set of Hebrew blessings that Jewish law prescribes following a meal that includes at least an ounce or more of bread.

bimah. A raised platform of the synagogue, on which stands the desk from which the Torah is read.

bubbe. Grandma (Yiddish).

Chabad. The Hasidic movement founded by the Alter Rebbe, Rabbi Schneur Zalman of Liadi (1745-1812).

chuppah. The canopy beneath which Jewish marriage ceremonies are performed.

challah. A loaf of fine bread baked in honor of the Sabbath and festivals, often braided.

Crown Heights. The neighborhood in Brooklyn, New York, that is the world headquarters of Chabad Lubavitch.

Golden Medina. Yiddish phrase, meaning golden land, referring to the United States as a land of opportunity.

haimish. Homey, cozy, unpretentious; or artificial. It comes from Yiddish *heymish.*

Kiddish. Ceremonial blessing pronounced over wine in a Jewish home or synagogue on a holy day.

kittel. A white robe, usually made of cotton, which traditionally a Jewish man wears first on his wedding day and afterward on certain Jewish holidays, such as Rosh Hashanah, Yom Kippur, and Passover, and ultimately as a burial shroud.

mensch. A decent and responsible human being, someone of noble character.

minyan. A quorum of ten men needed to say specific prayers

mishegoss. A Yiddish word meaning crazy or senseless behavior or activity. (Also meshugaas, mishegaas.)

mitzvot. Commandments in the Torah (the Hebrew Bible, which some Christians refer to as "The Old Testament").

Lubavitch. A townlet in White Russia, which was the center of the Chabad Hasidism from 1813-1915. Its name became a synonym for the Chabad movement.

rebbe. A saintly Torah leader (literally, "my teacher") who serves as a spiritual guide to his followers, who are known as Hasidim.

satori. The experience of awakening ("enlightenment") or apprehension of the true nature of reality.

Shabbos. Yiddish term for the Jewish Sabbath.

Torah. Literally, "lesson, instruction": The Five Books of Moses; also refers to the entire Jewish Law, including the Talmud and other sacred literature. The Torah is composed of both the revealed and the mystical teachings. According to Hasidic philosophy, the Torah is the "Blueprint of Creation" and literally the "Will and Wisdom of G-d."

yarmulke. Also called a *kipah* or *skullcap*, it is a small, brimless cap worn by Orthodox Jewish males, also worn by most Conservative and some Reform Jewish males during prayer.

yichud. A Hebrew word; according to Jewish religious law (halakha), yichud rules prohibit seclusion in a private area of a man and a woman who are not married to each other (excepting certain close relatives).

yud. A small letter in the Hebrew alphabet.

Questions for Discussion

1. How has the author's story changed your attitude toward mental illness?

2. The author writes about her experience as a patient with three different outpatient therapists. How did their styles differ?

3. What motivated the author to start taking lithium after refusing to take it six months earlier?

4. How would you explain why some of the author's coworkers—including counselors and therapists—stigmatized, shamed, or harassed the author for having a mental illness?

5. Who helped the author resolve her conflict about marrying, and how did they do it?

6. How were the author's challenges affected by those experienced by Mollie and Yetta?

7. What generational patterns may influence how you conduct your life?

8. How did the author benefit from exposure to Jewish people who practiced their religion more strictly than she was accustomed to?

9. How did the author benefit from mentors other than Hasidic rabbis?

10. What do you think of the author's response to her mother becoming a clown? How would you feel if your mother took up a practice that surprised or embarrassed you?

11. What stands out for you about the author's mother, Mollie, and their relationship?

12. Do you think Yetta would have had a different life if she was a young mother in the 1960s or later, when more safety nets (welfare, food stamps, housing assistance) existed?

13. Would Yetta have spent most of her life as a psychiatric inpatient if modern medications were available to decrease her symptoms of mental illness?

14. What traits of the author explain how she reversed a self-defeating dating pattern?

15. Do you think the anger workshop caused the author's first psychotic episode, or would it have happened anyway? What caused her subsequent episodes?

About the Author

 Marcia Naomi Berger (née Fisch), LCSW, is a psychotherapist who helps couples and others create fulfilling relationships. She also wants to help replace the stigma around mental illness with compassion, understanding, and respect. Berger wrote this memoir after decades of keeping her struggle with bipolar disorder a secret. She wants people with mental illness to know they are not alone and to make her story readily available to their family members, therapists, friends, and others.

The Bipolar Therapist shows Berger's conflict about marrying and its resolution. She became fascinated by how to keep a relationship thriving and shares this knowledge with clients in her private psychotherapy practice.

Berger lives in San Rafael, California. While employed by the City and County of San Francisco, she held senior-level positions in the fields of child welfare, alcoholism treatment, and psychiatry. She also served as executive director of a family service agency and as a lecturer at the University of California, San Francisco, School of Medicine.

She enjoys swimming, pickleball, Feldenkrais exercises, mahjong, bananagrams, and watching old Mary Tyler Moore television shows.

Berger is the author of *Marriage Meetings for Lasting Love* and *Marriage Minded: An A to Z Dating Guide for Lasting Love.* www.marcianaomiberger.com